# Clerical Culture

# Clerical Culture

## Contradiction and Transformation

### THE CULTURE
### OF THE DIOCESAN PRIESTS
### OF THE UNITED STATES
### CATHOLIC CHURCH

Michael L. Papesh

LITURGICAL PRESS
Collegeville, Minnesota

www.litpress.org

| 1 | 2 | 3 | 4 | 5 | 6 | 7 | 8 |
|---|---|---|---|---|---|---|---|

**Library of Congress Cataloging-in-Publication Data**

Papesh, Michael L., 1950–
    Clerical culture : contradiction and transformation : the culture of
the diocesan priests of the United States Catholic Church / Michael L.
Papesh.
       p.  cm.
    Includes bibliographical references and index.
    ISBN 0-8146-3001-4 (pbk. : alk. paper)
    1. Catholic Church—United States—Clergy.   I. Title.

BX1912.P255  2004
262'.14273—dc22

              2003018786

*To the Trinity,*

*whose love brings me into being,*

*in thanksgiving*
*for the churches that have nourished me in that love:*

*my family*

*the Archdiocese of St. Paul and Minneapolis*
*and its Presbytery*

*the Diocese of Joliet-in-Illinois*
*and its Presbytery*

*and the monks of*
*St. Meinrad Archabbey*
*St. Procopius Abbey*
*St. John's Abbey*

# Contents

# Acknowledgments

This reflection about the life of the Catholic Church, and ordained life and ministry within it, emerges out of a lifetime of personal experience. In that very broad context, what follows is the gift of the personal support, critical insight, and abundant good gifts of many people. For all that has been I feel heartfelt gratitude.

To some, however, I owe a special debt.

Fr. Edward Estok and Fr. Thomas Dragga of the Diocese of Cleveland took a great risk in asking me to speak at their Presbyteral Assembly in 2002. Their generous trust, Bishop Anthony Pilla's hope-filled vision, and the Cleveland Presbytery's gracious reception began a process that culminated in this book. God called me to this ministry from Cleveland.

In the summer of 2002, my folks, Mary Jean and Joseph Arado, were kind enough to let me spend hours on the computer at their Colorado ranch rather than spend vacation time with them. Their insightful comments on content and style were of enormous help in the early stages and set the course for what was to follow. As I read text out loud and quibbled over words and ideas, they gave me the long-suffering kindness only family can offer.

Back in St. Paul, Dr. Kate Lally deepened and expanded my understanding of sexuality and my perspective on sexual abuse and its consequences in family systems and in the Church. Her respect for the dignity of the victim, her compassion for the perpetrator, and her passionate commitment to see effective change in the Church remain an inspiration to me. Dr. Russ Connors and Dr. William McDonough from the College of St. Catherine offered both their moral theology expertise and personal reflections, which helped me focus much more clearly on what could and could not reasonably be said in the text. Russ's meticulous commentary was especially useful. Fr. Kevin McDonough offered a characteristically challenging perspective because of his long experience of being the Chancery official for St. Paul and Minneapolis who has ministered to victims of abuse and dealt with priest perpetrators and the surrounding legal processes. Sr. Marian Walstrom, c.s.j., along with the pastoral staff of Holy Spirit Parish, Dr. Mary Adrian, Joy Biedrcyzki, Dorothy Paulson, and Dr. Mary Seidel, generously and patiently helped deepen my insight into the relationship between the ordained and the rest of the Church because of their long years of experience as women in church ministry.

I am grateful to my brother Roger, my cousin Bill Nolan, my friends Fr. John Bauer and Fr. Paul Jaroszeski, my colleague Deacon Bill Umphress, and my spiritual director Fr. Richard Rice, s.j., for their years and years of patient listening, kindly encouragement, keen discernment, sharp critique, and gifted storytelling.

Thanks to the enthusiasm and expertise of Dennie Scott, the text that follows is considerably shorter and more focused than it might have been. What would the literary world be without English majors! My friend Jodi Auvin offered critical assurances at difficult times in the writing process, and to her I owe the final polish of the text. Without Jodi's encouragement the work would still be a lode of megabytes in a hard drive. Many thanks to Renee Svard for her work on the change grid in appendix 4.

Whatever is to be said of ecclesial culture as a whole, the experience of church, like politics, is profoundly local. I wish to thank the parishioners of St. Joseph's Slovenian Parish in Joliet, Illinois, for introducing me as a child to the multi-layered and richly textured community life that parish can be. The Benedictine monks of three abbeys, especially St. Meinrad Archabbey, have enflamed in me a passionate love for the Church and a hunger to grasp the vast sweep of its tradition. I am forever grateful. I also wish to thank the parishioners and staff of Holy Spirit in St. Paul. Their daily prayer and loving support since 1993, together with their serenity even when the pastor was off writing in his study, have contributed immeasurably to what follows.

But above all else, in the end, who is like God!

Michael Leo Papesh
frmichaelpapesh@yahoo.com

# Part One:
# Focusing the Issues

# 1. A Personal Story

I spent the spring of 2002 riveted to the daily newspaper and Catholic periodicals as reports piled up about the growing sexual abuse scandal in the Catholic Church. I grieved for the victims of sexual misconduct and their families, felt frustrated with some bishops and outraged at some priests. I could not let it go. The news hooked me completely. It hit home.

## A. SEXUAL ASSAULT AND ITS CONSEQUENCES

Plied with alcohol at a rectory dinner party with three fellow-seminarian friends and the pastor on a Saturday evening in 1969, I passed out. I was eighteen; it was the first time I had drunk too much. I woke in a dazed stupor some time later to find the priest on top of me. Reeling, I shortly passed out again. Sunday morning I woke up in my pajamas in bed. I had no idea how I got there. I could see no evidence from the behavior of my companions, especially the priest, indicating that what I thought had occurred had indeed happened. Confused, I asked one of my friends. He told the story of his pulling the priest off me and sending him out to put on a robe and distract the others while my friend clothed me and put me to bed.

I had no framework for comprehending the event. I felt ashamed, though, and my instinct was to assume, even if I was unclear about who was responsible for what, that it was wrong. So, upon returning to the seminary on Sunday, I went to one of the priests and asked him to hear my confession. He was a fresh PH.D. in psychology. Appalled at what I told him, and casting aside his typical reserve, he blurted out, "Surely the man is culpable!" For my penance, however, he asked me to pray Psalm 51. I had to look it up. The penance was the most unusual and the stiffest that, to this day, I have ever received.[1] The experience left me in a muddle of

---

[1] Commonly referred to as "The *Miserere*," its first words in Latin, Psalm 50/51 is a penitential psalm of nineteen verses beginning, "Have mercy on me, O God, according to your steadfast love; according to your abundant mercy blot out my transgressions."

double messages—somehow still wounded, yet forgiven; having heard the priest strongly blamed, yet feeling myself somehow at fault, a greater sinner than I had been before. The one thing I knew for sure—at least in the way I thought of it at the time—was that I never wanted to become so lonely that I would sexually seize someone. This conviction, and the fear underneath it, dominated my life for over a decade and a half.

The year following the sexual assault, I left diocesan priesthood seminary study to become a candidate for monastic community life at St. Meinrad Archabbey in southern Indiana. I saw in the monks' life intellectual breadth, gorgeous liturgy, and joyous personal commitment. The monastic community looked like a large family who cared for each other well. I thought monastic life would be exactly the protection I sought from loneliness. My motives, however, could not sustain me in the reality of the ups and downs of closed community life. After nearly four years, feeling keenly both emotional emptiness and the fragility of being a hothouse flower—I had entered seminary at thirteen—I left the monastery to live with friends in Minnesota and make my way in the world. I was twenty-five and had spent nearly half my life in seminary and monastic formation.

Over the next months I fell into chronic slight fatigue, a form of depression in which I napped all the time. I did factory and employment agency work for a while but came to understand that I needed more meaning in my life than this work gave me. So, after some searching, I sought out lay ministry in the Church, ultimately spending five years as a campus minister: two years at the then College of St. Thomas in St. Paul and three years as director of Campus Ministry at St. John's University, Collegeville. I look back on these as wonderful years of finally growing up. Life in ministry was rich and full. I had the benefit of many healing friendships that I enjoy today. God's gifts were lavish and abundant.

When I passed thirty, though, I knew I desired something more. But what? Unsure, I went home, back to Illinois where I was born, and to a monastery there, St. Procopius Abbey. For six months I prayed with the monks, did manual labor, and waited on God's call. Through the monks' generosity, my friends' faithfulness, my family's care, and God's inscrutable work, I was clearly and compellingly called to ordained ministry in Minnesota. I had wrestled with God, and God called me hobbling back to the only way of life I truly feared: diocesan priesthood. I desired it only because I was absolutely convinced that God desired it for me.

Ordained at age thirty-two in 1983, I found that God continued to push me into wholeness as a human being. Through God's healing power offered me by and through many wonderful people, I have come to face, among other things, the fact of being sexually assaulted and its consequences in my life. I know well the anger, grief, fear, confusion, mistakes, remorse, and hope that marks, for one who has been assaulted, the stumbling journey toward clear sexual boundaries, genuine personal intimacy, and sexual health. I have come at the same time to be whole-heartedly committed to celibacy. Yet the newspaper stories about the Archdiocese of Boston and other places across the country in 2002 surfaced in me a fervent desire to see sexual abuse and its causes eradicated in the Church, literally dug up from the very roots.

## B. INSPIRATION AND OPPORTUNITY

In April 2002 my interior churning led me to submit an article about clerical culture to *America* magazine.[2] Writing it was a seminal event, expressing deep concerns and root convictions I had long held but had rarely articulated even to my closest friends. The words poured up and out from deep within me.

In response to the article, a chancery official from the Diocese of Cleveland asked if I would be willing to make an October presentation about the clerical culture to a convocation of the Cleveland priests. Bishop Anthony M. Pilla had expressed to his staff his concern about the clerical culture and thought it would be a helpful topic to address directly with the priests. I consented to give the talk. Two weeks later the same official called back to ask if I could recommend someone for a follow-up talk to reflect on how we priests might change the clerical culture. I offered to do that talk as well. Because I was an unknown quantity, I promised to have the full texts of both talks on his desk by the first week of August so he might have time to find another speaker if he wished. During the month of writing that followed, the words welled up in me from deep within. Ultimately, I gave both talks to the Cleveland priests' convocation on October 28, 2002.

### i. The Situation in the Diocese of Cleveland

The Diocese of Cleveland experienced the sexual abuse scandal much like many other dioceses. Cleveland had twenty-eight priests accused of sexual misconduct; fifteen had remained active. The active priests had,

---

[2] Michael L. Papesh, "Farewell to the Club," *America* (vol. 186, no. 16, May 16, 2002) 7–10.

long in the past, admitted to some form of sexual abuse, been treated for it, and then returned to ministry. According to diocesan practice, these priests had been returned after the diocesan review board had reflected upon and discussed doctors' reports and, in some cases, after receiving permission from victims. A peculiarity of the Cleveland situation, however, was that it was widely suspected in diocesan circles that someone released inside information to the media.

In February 2002 Cleveland's only newspaper, *The Plain Dealer*, invited Bishop Pilla to meet with them. They told him they had the names and details of the fifteen priests still active in ministry, and they intended to publish them as a local interest expansion on *The Boston Globe* stories. All fifteen were admitted violators of young people.

The first public allegation brought against an active priest occurred at the beginning of Holy Week. One week later, Easter Monday, April 1, Fr. Donald Rooney was accused. He disappeared the following night and was found dead in his car of a self-inflicted gunshot wound on Thursday morning. In the midst of this national news, the Cuyahoga County prosecutor subpoenaed the diocese for its files. That same day *The Plain Dealer* began its detailed stories about the fifteen priests. In response to this swirl of events, the priests of the diocese became deeply anxious, presuming Bishop Pilla had released the diocesan files when, in fact, the material had been obtained by *The Plain Dealer* from "another source."

The Diocese of Cleveland, the eleventh largest in the United States, won national attention initially because of the suicide of Father Rooney and then because of the false report that the bishop had released to the media all its files. The status of the accused in Cleveland also won attention. One was the rector of the cathedral, another was the head of their judicial tribunal—both priests with significant public responsibilities. In addition, Cleveland Auxiliary Bishop A. James Quinn attracted national attention because of his involvement in the Canonical Affairs Committee of the National Conference of Catholic Bishops at the time it dealt with the sexual abuse question during the early 1990s. Moreover, Bishop Pilla, voted in 2000 the third most powerful man in Cleveland, was a past-president of the National Conference of Catholic Bishops. The Diocese of Cleveland came under intense scrutiny during spring 2002.

### ii. The Diocese's Response

Bishop Pilla's response to the pressure was threefold. First, he met with the victims of sexual abuse. This connection with the people's outrage changed his perspective. Immediately afterward he publicly took responsibility for the priests' behavior and the diocese's response to sexual misconduct. He then set to work to change what he admitted to be his own wrong-mindedness in the past and that of others. Then, after the United States Catholic Conference of Bishops meeting in Dallas that June, Bishop Pilla placed all fifteen active priest-perpetrators on administrative leave. A native of Cleveland who had spent his whole life in the diocese, Bishop Pilla describes this period in his life as one of "gut pain." Third, he held listening sessions with all of the priests of the diocese, which were transforming for him. As he told the priests of Cleveland on the convocation day:

> Part of my journey from emptiness to redemptive hope was listening to you. In listening to you I knew that you were experiencing much of what I was feeling. My sense of isolation, helplessness, and literally doom were undone piece by piece with each of those sessions. I heard you say that you felt it too, that you were feeling lost too, that you too were struggling to imagine how we would ever again soar from the low place we find ourselves. In almost every one of those eight sessions I heard somebody say something that I wish I had the freedom to say. I heard you saying that you were thinking, feeling, aching and searching just like I was. And in that I found hope. I heard your concerns, your fears, your angers, questions and resentments. I heard your pleas for better communication, more effective use of the media, more education about sexual abuse and boundaries, more involvement in the means of decision-making. I agreed with all of that . . . .[3]

The listening sessions themselves garnered an enormous amount of material from the priests about their perspective and feelings.

Building on the priests' responses, the bishop and his staff structured a day of presentation and reflection for the priests on September 23, 2002. It featured Fr. Steven Rosetti, director of the St. Luke's Institute in Silver Springs, Maryland, a treatment center for priests who have sexually offended, and Judith Wood, a member of Bellflower Center, a treatment and advocacy center for abuse victims, who helped the priests understand how victims feel. This day was followed by the traditional

---

[3] This quotation is taken from the unpublished Anthony M. Pilla, "Bishop Pilla's Address to the Convocation." This text of this address, presented on October 28, 2002, to the priests of Cleveland, was offered through the courtesy of Fr. Edward Estok, then the bishop's secretary.

fall convocation day for priests on October 28, 2002. It included a pre-convocation presentation on shame by psychologist Brian Frawley, PH.D., the night before. The keynotes for the day itself were my two presentations: one about the clerical culture and its contradictions, the other about how priests might transform the clerical culture.

The convocation was framed to be strategic. In response to the second talk challenging priests to change clerical culture, over three hundred priests gathered in small groups to answer two questions: What were their greatest hopes roused by the talk? What were the greatest concerns that rose in them because of the talk? The results of these sessions were distributed to the priests that evening.[4]

The next morning the priests were divided into five groups, each moderated by a priest chosen by the bishop and his staff. The groups were assigned a double task. First, they were asked to agree on the three uppermost concerns they wished to see addressed regarding clerical culture, one each under the headings holiness, love, and justice. Second, each was to elect a member of the group to serve with its moderator on a task force of ten priests that would tackle all of the issues raised by the five groups.[5] All of the items surfaced in the groups were brought before the whole assembly. Then, in the final Eucharist, Bishop Pilla called the members of the task force forward and formally, ritually, charged them to their task. Within the ritual he asked the whole body of priests to publicly pledge their support to the task force and their cooperation with its work. The priests as a body did so resoundingly.

This experience was stunning. A courageous bishop, with touching humility, publicly accepted responsibility for his former, faulty vision of priest sexual abuse and the diocesan response to it. Because of his leadership, the presbytery of the diocese gathered to ponder forthrightly the contradictory circumstances of clerical culture and what they might do to change it. The bishop and presbytery together then publicly and ritually committed themselves to a specific course of constructive action to change clerical culture in their diocese. In the words of Bishop Pilla:

> . . . the changeless truth of our priesthood can be understood and lived in a radically different way. In fact, it must be. We can re-invent ourselves as Christian leaders of hope without losing the priesthood of Jesus Christ. The priesthood can be special without being privileged. Priestly life can be fulfilling without being opulent. The priest can be respected without being

---

[4] See Appendix 1.
[5] See Appendix 2.

feared. Priests can be united and mutually supportive without being arrogant and aloof. The Church community and hierarchy can be faithful to its priests without creating a dependent or privileged class. These categories of renewal and others that you are imagining need to be part of our movement forward.[6]

The Holy Spirit has gifted the church of Cleveland, in all of its pain, with a season of hope.[7] Perhaps the Holy Spirit of God is longing likewise to gift the whole church in the United States.

## C. THE SUBJECT

Many writers since 2002 have suggested that the clerical culture in the Roman Catholic Church in the United States is a major accomplice in the sexual misconduct scandal. I agree with them. It is the context of all the other causes, and it nurtures and nourishes them. Consequently, I am convinced that the church in the U.S. needs to come to terms with the clerical culture: to name what it is, understand how it works, critique it, and then begin the hard work of cultural change. This conviction has led to this book.

I am no anthropologist, no sociologist, no ethnographer, no expert of any sort. I am, however, an observer, student, and continually amazed ponderer of life in the Church, in ministry and before God, who has lived since 1964 in and around the clerical culture. Therefore, I seek within these pages to describe the culture, its history and contradictions, and some possibilities for its transformation. My passion for the subject is stoked by three concerns.

Much of what I have seen in the clerical culture over the years has left me feeling ill at ease. I was "a lifer" in the seminary, entering at thirteen, and a "delayed vocation," ordained out of the normal course at thirty-two. I have been a monk and a lay minister. In parish settings I have been an associate pastor, a pastor, and a weekend assistant. I spent seven years as a seminary spiritual director at both the college and

---

[6] Bishop Anthony M. Pilla, *op. cit.*

[7] In its February 28, 2003, edition, *The New York Times* wrote that a Cuyahoga County grand jury had investigated accusations against 145 Cleveland priests and indicted one. It also investigated accusations against 315 laypersons in the diocese's employ. The Diocese of Cleveland could not account for the gap between its figures of 28 accused priests, 15 active, and the grand jury's number. At that time the diocese had not yet set up its Dallas-mandated review board. It was also legally challenging the opening to the public of the grand jury investigative files.

graduate school levels. Over the years I have done chancery committee volunteer work in the areas of continuing education for priests, priestly life and ministry, the presbyteral council, and the priests' personnel board. This experience, coupled with having lived in four Midwest dioceses and three monastic communities, has given me the opportunity not only to see the inner workings of the clerical culture but also to become sensitive to some of the contradictions that ensnare the ordained. They are signs of cultural decay near the heart of the church and of spiritual malaise among the ordained. I feel compelled to write and talk about these things so they might be changed.

Second, as a pastor I have become aware that the people with and among whom I serve know very little—next to nothing—about the clerical culture. They were deeply shaken by what became public during 2002, even as they remained faithful. They seek assurance that the institutional Church will do everything in its power to see to it that sexual exploitation never happens again. Adequate assurance has not been forthcoming, however. Moreover, because many parish ministry staff people and laity have become newly conscious of how much they do not know about how the Church operates day by day, they are frustrated and vaguely alarmed by the suspicion that they have even less power than they thought. I know they are right. Certainly the laity of the Church need to understand the clerical culture much more fully and to hold the ordained accountable for continuing to grow in authentic faith and hope, holiness, love, and justice for the sake of fulfilling the Church's mission in the world.

Third, with and for my brother priests and bishops, I feel grief. The vast numbers of healthy priests are compromised by the ill and confused. Guileless and open priests are thwarted by the manipulative and blockheaded. Sincere and faithful priests are undone by the secretive and exploitative. The gospel ministry of Jesus Christ is being assaulted on many sides, priestly ministry is being tarnished and its effectiveness diminished, all because of circumstances that the church in the United States could change, and which many priests and bishops want to change. Perhaps exposing the spiritual malaise of the clerical culture openly, publicly, for church-wide reflection will help them focus their desires and motivate them—us—to act.

The change we seek, though, has significant structural elements. Thus the question "Where do we begin?" is daunting. Perhaps this writing can offer some stimulus toward the answer to that question.

What follows is not an angry rant. Throughout my life, before and within ordained ministry, I have been as dazzled by the clerical culture as

I have been put off by it, as healed within it as I have been hurt by it. I have respect for both the great power and the enormous unused potential of it. The experience underneath the three concerns above means, therefore, that what you read I badly need to read as well, and when my index finger points, I know keenly that three fingers point back. So, what follows is much less a clarion call to tear down the walls of the great bastion called "church" than it is a longing, hope-filled whimper at the door to reform of the clergy that I fervently pray will be opened wide in the church of the United States.

# 2. The Problem

During the summer of 2002, the investigative staff of *The Boston Globe* published a book about its exposé of the Archdiocese of Boston's handling of priestly sexual misconduct. Entitled *Betrayal: The Crisis in the Catholic Church,* the authors focus on a central problem American Catholics are groping to understand. Paraphrasing *Betrayal,* that problem might be stated as a question:

> . . . what [is] it about [our] Church that [has] enabled more than fifteen hundred priests to molest minors and [has] caused numerous bishops to shuffle problem priests from parish to parish rather than fire them or turn them over to prosecutors[?].[1]

This question, if addressed, takes us inexorably into the heart of the matter.

## B. THE CAUSES OF THE SCANDAL

The reasons for the sexual misconduct scandal are many and, like the plateau formations of the high New Mexico desert, thoroughly blended. Sorting the layers is like excavation. Still, layers are clearly evident. We have read about them at least indirectly. Instinctively we recognize them when we see them. For whatever the 2004 report from the bishops conference offers as causes for the scandal, nine of these layers are especially important.

One layer is *pathology.* Pedophilia and ephebophilia are distinct pathologies.[2] Pedophilia is sexual orientation toward a child. The pedophile is usually a male, and the attraction may be toward a male or female child. Ephebophilia is sexual orientation toward a teen. The ephebophile may be male or female, and the attraction may be toward a male or female teen. The preponderance of cases we have read about are cases of

---

[1] *The Boston Globe* investigative staff, *Betrayal: The Crisis in the Catholic Church* (Boston: Little, Brown, 2002) 184.

[2] The best article I have seen on this issue is Melvin C. Blanchette and Gerald D. Coleman, "Priest Pedophiles," *America* (vol. 186, no. 13, April 22, 2002) 18–21. Also see Joseph J. Guido, "The Importance of Perspective: Understanding the Sexual Abuse of Children by Priests," *America* (vol. 186, no. 11, April 1, 2002) 21–23.

male attraction to male teens. These clinically known and diagnosable conditions in particular former priests, for instance, John Goeghan and Paul Shanley, are one cause of the scandal.

Some commentators have included homosexual orientation in the pathology mix. They have done so particularly because they connect same sex ephebophilia with homosexuality. However, there is no clinical connection between the two. Second, in spite of some bias to the contrary, homosexuality is rarely regarded among psychologists and psychiatrists as pathology.[3] The church's perspective, of course, is quite wary.

Another cause for the scandal is *moral culpability*, sin, on the part of the perpetrators. Some clergy, like Auxiliary Bishop James Murray of New York, chose to have an affair in spite of their celibate commitment. These adult-to-adult sexual relationships on the scandal list have received relatively little attention in the media. Nonetheless, they are worth noting because they have made the national press.

Both of the above reasons themselves have a cause. The *seminary system* in which most of the perpetrators were formed was sexually repressive. That was not its intention. The seminary's aim was the formation of young men toward celibacy. Its effect was sexual repression, typically from the moment the student entered the door. Some entered at age thirteen. The structure of seminary life and formation in a closed, all-male, community environment nervous about the very subject of sex often kept seminarians from having to face their own and others' sexuality.[4] For example, one graduate school professor was known to shut the classroom transom, close the windows, and pull the shades before he began his academic lecture in moral theology entitled *"De Sexto."* Consequently, the inner movements of sexual drive were either repressed utterly, dealt with secretly, or acted out later. Father Goeghan's story—a mild, adolescent adult eating ice cream and giggling to win victims—though it is exceptional, offers an especially tragic glimpse into what repression giving way to perversion looks like, evidently without adult moral, intellectual, or emotional comprehension of reality.

---

[3] The April 18, 2003, issue of *National Catholic Reporter* noted that the Vatican had gathered eight experts across the world, none Catholic, to discuss the issue. The experts agreed that homosexuality was a risk factor in ordaining priests, but all agreed that it was not a cause for sexual abuse. *NCR* speculated the proposed document that would exclude homosexual men from ministry, therefore, would likely not appear. In March three subcommittees of the United States Conference of Catholic Bishops met with experts to discuss the implications for the U.S. church of the Vatican's issuing such a document.

[4] See Paul E. Dinter, *The Other Side of the Altar: One Man's Life in the Catholic Priesthood* (New York: Farrar, Straus and Giroux, 2003) 32–35, for a detailed illustration of this point.

Yet another reason for the scandal is *lack of knowledge* about the real issues. In many instances what we now know to be pathology was thought by bishops and chancery officials to be moral failure and therefore correctable. In light of the Gospel, apologies were sincerely received and forgiveness sincerely offered. Sometimes the real issue was unclear. In the case of sexual assault against me, for instance, the bishop and I both assumed when it was confronted in 1975 that the bottom-line issue was the priest's alcoholism, not the assault. The priest was returned to ministry. It was not until the early-to-mid-1980s that the church in the United States began to comprehend the uncorrectable pathological issues involved in some cases of sexual misconduct. A number of bishops were slower than others to accept the facts, and a number were slower than others to establish appropriate diocesan procedures.

The *paternalism* of bishops toward priests is another cause of the sexual misconduct scandal. Cardinal Law's assignment and post-treatment letters to Fathers Shanley and Goeghan are amazing witness to how some bishops take their responsibility to care for their priests to the point of what seems flagrant indulgence. Surely the Cardinal thought he was being compassionate and giving his priests the benefit of the doubt. In hindsight, many would judge him to have been grossly misguided as he cooed over moral monsters; for many, John Goeghan's ultimate fate of murder in prison raises anguishing questions about the consequences of paternalism. Still, bishop paternal care for priests is a pattern across the country, and it is a cause for the scandal.

A bishop's instinct for *protection of the church* as institution is another cause. Wordless removal of a priest from a parish, withholding information from the next parish and other dioceses, and confidentiality agreements are all symptoms of institutional self-protection. Sometimes this instinct for self-preservation motivated political caution as well. For instance, to have moved strongly against a widely-known and admired priest, like the side-burned, motorcycle-riding, young Father Shanley in the 1960s, would have been to risk political repercussions among priests and people that would have created some havoc in the Boston church. Though hindsight would judge otherwise, handling things silently surely seemed in some moments to ensure smoother sailing.

*Loyalty* to priests they knew for a lifetime was also a cause of the scandal. Bishops and chancery officials had to confront people whom they had known since age thirteen, thought they knew well, and loved and respected. These long-standing relationships among the ordained, and the grave difficulty of being tough with someone whom you have accepted, respected, and even admired, considerably slowed bishop and chancery action over the years.

*Cowardice* is yet another cause. We have read over and over again in newspapers about chancery officials who had grave reserve—or seemed to have had it—and yet went ahead with placing perpetrators in parishes against their better judgment because of what they thought or knew the bishop or "the system" expected. This moral failure has left a sword hanging over the heads of former chancery officials, especially diocesan bishops across the country who were former Boston auxiliary bishops.

Yet another reason for the scandal is priests *taking advantage* of the gracious, generous, nigh boundary-free trust lay people have had toward the ordained. Priest perpetrators took advantage by gaining access to young people for dark motives and giving perverse orders that they knew would be unquestioningly obeyed. Bishops took advantage by putting off victims and their advocates with promises they had little intention of keeping or by negotiating or commanding silence when the chips were down.

Other factors that contribute to the causes of the scandal are chancery office *inefficiency,* pastor *failure to supervise* an associate, and the terrible awkwardness of *doubt/denial,* wondering if what you are suspecting is going on can really be true. *Attorney acquiescence* to church demands, *church acquiescence* to attorney suggestion, and a *piecemeal approach* to cases rather than with the broad or long view are also factors. Human and institutional *pride* as well as personal *vanity* and *hopelessness* also figure into the patterns that our national church has witnessed.

The nine causes for the sexual misconduct scandal listed above, as well as the other factors, and likely others still,[5] are so thoroughly enmeshed that no one factor dominates the rest. A commonality, however, exists among all the reasons for the sexual misconduct scandal: they are sustained by a culture in which they have been allowed to continue. That clerical culture, the primary professional context for Latin Rite diocesan presbyters and bishops in the United States, is a primary answer to the question: why the sexual misconduct scandal in the United States? Clerical culture in itself, therefore, must be examined for its contribution to the scandal.

---

[5] Archbishop O'Malley of Boston adds that another cause for the scandal may have been the time of turmoil after Vatican II in both the Church and American society. He suggests that some started to act out when the supports "for religious life, for asceticism, for virtue" were taken away. See James Martin, s.j., "'To Love and to Pray': A Conversation with Boston's Archbishop Sean O'Malley," *America* (vol. 186, no. 13, October 27, 2003) 8–10.

## C. WHAT IS *CULTURE*?

Historian and theologian Thomas O'Meara, o.p., writes, "If the blood of the church is history, the flesh of the community of Christ is culture."[6] Culture is all about the forms of an organization's life, whether that be the family, the corporation, or the nation state.

The definition of *culture* used in what follows comes from George Mendenhall's *Ancient Israel's Faith and History: An Introduction to the Bible in Context.* Mendenhall defines culture as "a meaningful arrangement of technology (the means by which people provide for material needs), society (people's relationships), and ideology (people's way of thinking, including religion).[7]

Culture, by definition, is a larger reality than the persons within it. We humans bear responsibility for culture's formation and continuance, yet the whole is greater than the sum of its parts. For instance, at the end of August 2002, media across the country wrote about the then new $189 million, three-thousand seat Our Lady of the Angels Cathedral in Los Angeles. In what seemed to be offered and received as a statement of humility, Cardinal Roger Mahony remarked that he personally wishes to be forgotten for his role as the cathedral's builder. His name will appear in the cathedral only on his crypt in the mausoleum. Many articles noted at the same time that crypts, which fund cathedral upkeep, sell for $50,000 each. Cardinal Mahony evidently saw no incongruity between his desire to be forgotten and the outlay of $150,000 for crypts for himself and his parents who are interred there. Culture is bigger than those who comprise it and blinds them to its contradictions.

Culture is also an evolving reality. For instance, clerical culture today is different from what it was in the 1950s. Then the parish likely had an older, single woman who lived in the rectory and cooked, cleaned, and did laundry for two or three priests. She also, in many cases, ran the parish because she was the gatekeeper to the pastor. Today many priests live alone in multi-room rectories. Some have offices and meeting rooms in them; others are for the priest alone. Many live in their own home, town house, or apartment. The priest himself typically cooks, does laundry, and maintains the house.

---

[6] Thomas F. O'Meara, *Theology of Ministry* (Mahwah, N.J.: Paulist Press, 1999) 23.

[7] George Mendenhall, ed. Gary Herion, *Ancient Israel's Faith and History: An Introduction to the Bible in Context* (Louisville: Westminster John Knox Press, 2001) 1.

## D. WHAT IS *CLERICAL* CULTURE?

What do we mean by *clerical* culture? Many bishops and priests know the answer only intuitively. Whether they despise it, thrive on it, or something in-between, the clerical culture is the medium in which most of the ordained live significant portions of their lives. Like fish in water, most bishops, priests, and laity take clerical culture unreflectively for granted. Any ten Catholics asked for a description of clerical culture would offer widely disparate perspectives. Yet, clerical culture is precisely the constellation of relationships and the universe of ideas and material reality in which diocesan priests and bishops exercise their ministry and spend their lives.

The culture of the priest who is a professed religious coincides only insofar as he works in a diocesan institution and participates in diocesan culture. The diocesan clerical culture, however, is likely secondary to that of his religious order's or congregation's culture.[8] The subculture of the bishops as a group, though arising out of the clerical culture and presiding over it, is not considered here in itself. That task belongs to some courageous bishop. In what follows, the bishop is considered only as head of the diocesan clerical culture. The subculture of the contemporary permanent deacon is tangential to clerical culture and so is also excluded from consideration.

Although it must be readily acknowledged that each of the 195 Catholic dioceses in the United States has its own subculture among the ordained, what follows broadly describes the major elements common to the culture of the diocesan priests of the Latin Rite of the Roman Catholic Church in the United States.

## E. THE TASK BEFORE US

It is critically important to do the hard work of trying to understand the clerical culture, especially its more problematic elements. We must do so in order to address this culture's spiritual malaise: its clear failure to provide the kind of health, balance and support the Church requires for accomplishing its mission. We need to ask and answer complex questions:

---

[8] One of the significant elements of Archbishop Sean Patrick O'Malley's appointment to Boston is that he is a religious and his being a Capuchin Franciscan is central to his personal self-understanding. For an archbishop to stand before his people in a Franciscan habit, indeed, to go so far as to wear the Franciscan hood outside his alb and chasuble at Mass even when he is wearing the miter, is a very strong symbol that this archbishop is an *outsider* to the clerical culture.

Where does the clerical culture come from historically? What are its constitutive elements? What are its extraneous elements? Which elements of it have led to the troubles in which we find ourselves today? Which are changeable and changing, and which are not? However imperfectly or incompletely, we as Church need to grapple with these questions.

Moreover, since culture is a given wherever human beings come together with common interests, goals, and tasks, we need to understand clerical culture and its history so we can intentionally shape it. Reshaping any culture is a long and difficult undertaking. For the clerical culture especially, it would require moving over time toward a new consensus among ordained and lay across the Church. Nonetheless, this kind of pondering, discussing, and changing is required if, in the future, the bishops and priests of the Catholic Church are to be respected and trusted as people of integrity, free to be about gospel ministry for the sake of the common good of the Church and the world.

The purpose of this book is to expose the clerical culture and some of its contradictions to the light of day and then point to some realistic ways in which ordained and lay people together might transform it. Hopefully, then, the church in the United States may come to regard its priests with more confidence and trust, and priests themselves may deepen the integrity of their witness by living in greater personal and spiritual health. After laying a historical groundwork of understanding, this work will review the theological underpinnings of the clerical culture. Then a narrative description of major elements of the clerical culture will follow, along with eleven contradictions in which the clerical culture is caught. The third section sketches an essentially spiritual vision for cultural transformation, for what ordained ministry can and must be in our age.

Some of the clerical culture's elements have remained in continuity since the rise of the distinction between lay and ordained. What we, the living, have experienced of it in the United States comes largely from the triumphal era of Catholicism (Pius IX to Pius XII) transposed across the sea to an immigrant church, with a strong, Irish twist that comes from the dominant national heritage of both bishops and priests in the United States for the last 150 years. This mix expanded and grew within the context of the dynamic culture of the United States: westward driving, affluent, mobile, consumerist, individualist, secular-Protestant, democratic republican. Thus, the clerical culture we have today among diocesan presbyters in the United States is, in many respects, unique within the universal Church and still quite potent.

The task before the church in the United States is enormous. It is no less than the transformation of how we do priesthood in the Catholic

Church—institutional change on a grand scale. The inherent mystery, ancient traditions, hierarchical structure, papal allegiance, and general social effectiveness of the Church leaves larger American society deeply suspicious of it. Some elements of our society are eager to undercut the Church and work out their own agendas against it. It is also true that invincible blindness in the face of reality, fierce opposition in the face of privilege, and a habit of self-protection are all around us within the Church. Nonetheless, the work toward transformation of the clerical culture is a Godly one, with abundant precedent across the Church's history. Transformation is a mission for the ages that we must accomplish here and now in the United States for the sake of the Gospel and the ever-greater effectiveness of the ministry of Jesus Christ in our midst.

As I overheard one priest say in Cleveland, Ohio, in October 2002, "You didn't think some documents written in the 1960s at Rome would reform the priesthood, did you? The sexual misconduct scandal—now that will do it!!" I couldn't agree more.

### F. THE BOTTOM LINE

Jesus has a powerful exchange with his disciples that needs to govern all of Christian life.

> When Jesus went into the region of Caesarea Philippi he asked his disciples, "Who do people say the Son of Man Is?" They replied, "Some say John the Baptist, others Elijah, still others Jeremiah or one of the prophets." He said to them, "And you, who do you say that I am?" (Matt 16:13-15).

Jesus' question proclaims that all Christians are the custodians and the guardians of the identity of Jesus for the Church and in the midst of the world. This sacred trust is intensified for the ordained in the Roman Catholic Church because people read the lives of the ordained closely to see what they reveal about the identity of Jesus.

To consider clerical culture is to consider the faithfulness of the ordained minister—and, ultimately, the faithfulness of the whole Church—to the corporate and personal call to be custodian and guardian of the identity of Jesus in the midst of the Church and the world. Therefore, underneath this probing of the clerical culture, and the transformation to which we need apply ourselves as a Church in our time, no question is more fundamental to the whole Church, particularly the ordained, than the one Jesus asks his disciples: And you, who do you say that I am? Across the ages, this question has always been most fundamental for the Church.

# 3. How the Clerical Culture Came to Be

## A. FATHOMING THE HISTORICAL DEPTHS BELOW THE WORD *CLERICAL*

A brief sketch of the evolution of the history of the clergy, the distinction between clergy and laity, and the evolving meaning of that distinction offers us a perspective from which to view some of the many layers underneath the word *clerical* and the term *clerical culture.*

By the end of the first century, which marks the near-end of the writing of the Christian Scriptures, certain persons in Christian communities across the Roman Empire come to form the *clerus,* a term designating the portion of the Lord, the Lord's share, the Lord's inheritance. The clerus is a group of people within the Christian faith community designated for spiritual and leadership functions. The roles and powers of the persons and groups who exercise these functions grow ever more differentiated and defined as the centuries progress, leading ultimately to what we know in our own time.

The first use of the word *laity,* in contrast to clergy, appears in Christian literature near the end of the first century in the "First Letter from Clement," sent by a member of the college of overseers from the church at Rome to the church at Corinth. It is another hundred years before another Clement, from Alexandria, uses the word again, and yet another hundred years before, in the *Didascalia Apostolorum,* we see the sense of separation that indicates that the clergy are somehow different from the laity. Though increasingly but only modestly significant for much of the first three centuries, the distinction between clergy and laity becomes fixed through the fourth and fifth centuries and remains today. What are the circumstances that bring about this distinction and make it useful for the Church? Though this long and complex history can be painted here only with the thinnest of brushes—what follows is the Sistine

Chapel painted in a matchbox—reviewing this history will help us grasp some of the depths of meaning underneath the clerical culture today.

## B. THE FIRST GENERATIONS

Until the mid-second century C.E. Christians shied away from the word *priest*[1] because it referred to functionaries in the cultic sacrifice worlds of the Jewish and pagan temples. Jesus is referred to as *priest* in the Letter to the Hebrews, but it is to make the point that he is the only priest, the high priest whose once-and-for-all sacrifice renders superfluous the sacrifices of all other priests. *Diakonia,* service, is the word used by Christians to designate ministry. The Christian assembly is a *diakonia* community gifted with the Holy Spirit of Jesus through baptism. These gracious gifts, or charisms, of the Spirit are intended for the service of the whole Christian community. Ministry in the ancient church is all about action, not cultic worship. Outward moving evangelization, preaching, teaching, and assembly leadership are the core ministries that constitute the Christian way of life. These actions, fundamentally the way a Christian lives his or her life, comprise the sacrifice, the liturgy, and the common priestly office of the whole people.

Roles of service are recognized within the faith community, but they vary from place to place. Apostle, prophet, and teacher are most prominent among some communities. Overseer, elder, and servant (bishop, presbyter, and deacon respectively) are most prominent among other communities. Ministry remains functional, service-oriented, diverse, fluid, and charismatic in the earliest generations. Flowing from the Holy Spirit's gifts in baptism, ministry emerges from a community's ongoing commitment to the harmonious working together of the whole for the sake of building the Kingdom. Specific roles emerge from a particular Christian assembly's recognition and selection of persons who have the right gifts.

Evidence suggests that presidency at the eucharistic table is likely given to senior, long-standing, exemplary, and fruitful leaders of the community—originally probably to the prophets but increasingly, as the

---

[1] The linguistic background for this word in English is complex. Our word *priest* refers back to what is meant by the Greek word *hiereus* and the Latin word *sacerdos,* both of which refer to one who held the cultic office of presidency and offering sacrifice in worship. The English word *priest* evolved, however, like the French *pretre,* from the Greek *presbyteros,* which means elder. In this text, the word *presbyter* will refer to the leadership role of elder, *priest* to the cultic functionary.

decades pass, to the overseers selected from among the elders (presbyters).[2]

Toward the end of the first century, when the ministries of overseer, elder, and servant rise more generally to the fore in most of the Christian communities, the precise contour of each ministry is unclear. The presbyters minister as a council-like group with the power to guide the community. The overseer seems to come from among the elders as the elected head of the presbyteral college.[3] He is selected to build up the community, hold it together, and assume responsibility for finances and sound doctrine. The referent for the deacons, however—an office held by men and women—is unclear. The word *diakonia* certainly refers to ministry in the community as a whole but might also describe the ministry of the overseer. We are simply unsure.[4]

## C. THE SECOND AND THIRD CENTURIES

The late first century through the early fourth century marks a gradual growth of the concept of *priest* in the Christian community.[5] This change, which moves at different rates in different ethnic groups across different cities among different kinds of people, occurs within a broad community context of enormous growth in the numbers of Christians— about half a million at the end of the first century expanding to some four to five million by the end of the third century. Martyrdom is another significant reality for the Christian community at this time. While martyrdom becomes the radical equalizer among all Christians through the third century, it also naturally coalesces the community's focus toward its leaders, its most likely martyrs.

---

[2] I use the term *overseer (episcopos)* for the English word bishop until that role resembles more of what we understand it to be today. I use the terms *elder (presbyteros)* and *presbyter* interchangeably.

[3] The overseers seem to be a college in the church at Rome, however, where no mention is made of a single overseer until the middle of the second century c.e.

[4] See Paul Bernier, *Ministry in the Church: A Historical and Pastoral Approach* (Mystic, Conn.: Twenty-Third Publications, 1992) 11–51, and Thomas F. O'Meara, o.p., *Theology of Ministry* (Mahwah, N.J.: Paulist Press, 1999) 35–79.

[5] The bulk of this chapter and the next follows Bernier, *op. cit.*, and O'Meara, *op. cit.* The time divisions vary from both at different points. O'Meara characterizes these periods as ones in which ministry was adapted to meet the Church's needs and was hugely successful. They also mark, however, the stages of the increasing contraction of ministry from apostolic times to the present.

During these centuries the communities meet in the upstairs rooms of people's houses for instruction and the eucharistic meal. As the community grows, the eucharistic meal and reflection on community life shift to rented guildhalls and apartment buildings. That, in turn, gives way in the third century to the community's reserving and decorating buildings for its own use. Concurrently during these centuries, the communities' evangelizing, preaching, and teaching orientation becomes more liturgically oriented toward the Sunday and feast day Eucharist as well as the celebration of the sacraments.

The late first-century and early second-century letters of Clement, one of the overseers in Rome, and of Ignatius, overseer of Antioch, witness to the increasing emphasis on the overseer, elected from among the elders as the full-time leader of the Christian community. This full-time ministry of leadership marks a significant change for the Church. The overseer is seen as the bond of unity for the community, the guarantor of its teaching, and the president of the presbyteral college. The deacon is the overseer's social minister, responsible for the administration, financial support, and practical care of the needy. The overseer and deacon are the main functional roles within the community, complimented by those of teacher, prophet, presbyter, deaconess, and widow. As time passes, however, the role of overseer comes to absorb the roles of teacher and prophet.

The primary leader in the life of the community presides over the Eucharist. The overseer becomes the ordinary presider over the Eucharist and the custodian of the eucharistic presidency during these centuries. The first mention of a presbyter presiding over the Eucharist is in a letter from the African overseer Cyprian in about 250. By the third century the overseer's role is starting to be cast in *priest* terms because the community wishes to have priests like other Roman religions do. The Old Testament priesthood gradually becomes the model of what the overseer role ought to be, which is exactly opposite of the first and second generation's understanding. The Christian community increasingly understands the Last Supper in sacrificial terms, and because the overseer presides at Eucharist, he comes to be understood in sacrificial *(priest)* terms.

Ordination begins in these centuries. *Ordinatio* is a technical term for the act of appointing functionaries to Roman civil office, which the Christians borrow. The overseer's own community, the presbyters and deacons, and the overseers of neighboring communities elect a presbyter to the leadership role of overseer. He is elected within, among, and for a particular ecclesial community. He is ordained by at least three neighboring overseers, followed by the community Eucharist. Across the Christian churches, this ceremony most often includes the laying on of hands. In some churches it consists of the candidate being seated on a chair. Both gestures are part of the ceremony in others of the churches.[6]

The important element of installation to this overseer ministry, however, is less the ritual surrounding it than the mandate of those who have elected the overseer to lead. By the fourth century the overseer is viewed as high priest within the community and is typically referred to as *sacerdos,* priest. The local overseer and the college of presbyters ordain new presbyters. The overseer alone ordains deacons for his service. Ministry is still viewed in essentially communal terms and arises from the particular community in which one serves. Overseers, presbyters, and deacons are all admitted into an *ordo,* or order, a word taken from Roman civil vocabulary indicating a social body distinct from others.

The presbyters during this period have status because they are senior in the faith and regarded as holy people, singular examples of faithfulness. As a college they advise the overseer, serve the community in certain judicial matters, and are the group from which the overseer is elected. Their role, to which the overseer and the college of presbyters ordain them, is less an office within the community than a status received because of the style of their life.

Increase of the Christian population, however, gradually demands that the presbyters assume some limited delegated leadership responsibility over smaller communities. The Roman civil government provides the administrative structure for helping keep the network of relationships clear, structuring the empire into large administrative units called *diokeseis,* using the Greek term (in English, "dioceses") and smaller units called *paroikia,* or "neighborhoods" (in English, "parishes"). It is during these centuries that the overseers come to resemble more clearly bishops as we know them today.

---

[6] It is interesting to note that, while the laying on of hands and invoking the Holy Spirit comes to be typical in ordinations, the precise gesture that ordains is not determined to be the laying on of hands until the apostolic constitution *Sacramentum ordinis* of Pope Pius XII in 1947. The exact gesture conferring ordination is unclear for some centuries because the question is not asked. When it is, the Scholastics favor the passing of the instruments of the order, the chalice of wine and paten of bread for the priest, for instance, as the ordaining moment. This moment is commonly considered to be the conferring moment until Pius XII in 1947.

## D. THE FOURTH AND FIFTH CENTURIES

All this early development poises the Christian community for the distinction between clergy and laity that arises after Constantine's Edict of Milan in 313 and Theodosius' making Christianity the state religion in 381. With these massive changes, the Christian population increases markedly (ten million of fifty million imperial citizens by 381), the Eucharist moves into imperial courthouses (the basilica churches), and bishops become appointed officials of the Roman Empire (mid-fourth century). Once Christianity becomes the state religion, it is responsible for safeguarding the empire, and the emperor is responsible for safeguarding the Church. Moving the capital from Rome to Constantinople in 330 reshapes church relationships even more as popes vie with patriarchs for influence with the emperor, linguistic and cultural differences between Rome and Constantinople become more pronounced, and consequent misunderstandings lead the Christian Church to increasing lack of communication and eventual split into East and West (1054). These factors lead to institutionalization in the Church and greater complexity of forms. Christian community office holders eventually become, both in service of the emperor and in service of a collapsed empire, civil servants. Against this backdrop the call to ministry is superseded for Christians in general by the call to virtuous life in and for the sake of the empire.

### i. Changes in the Roles of Presbyters and Bishops

By the time of the Council of Nicea in 325, the role of the presbyter is changing. As the century progresses, the bishop's power continues to increase as the population grows, and so the bishops increasingly send presbyters into the countryside around the metropolitan areas of the empire to take leadership of particular communities. The presbyters gradually become less and less the council that elects the bishop, offers him advice and adjudicates, and more and more the bishop's helpers, exchanging their independence for cult leadership as presiders over the Eucharist, which begins the movement toward their being understood increasingly in priestly terms. The shift to state religion also means that civil religious customs already in place are now imposed on the Christian churches, including exempting clerics from taxes and giving them an imperial salary.[7]

---

[7] The ordained eventually come to receive enough to live on in 1179 at the Third Lateran Council.

Throughout the fourth and into the fifth century, the leadership of the bishops grows to dominate the life of the Church and the state. The bishops become increasingly collegial as a body, taking on the mantle of the college of apostles for the whole of the Church. This is the age of the great theologian bishops: Athanasius of Alexandria (293–373), Hilary of Poitiers (315–367), Basil of Caesarea (329–379), Gregory Nazianzen (330–389), Gregory of Nyssa (335–394), Ambrose of Milan (339–397), John Chrysostom of Constantinople (347–407), Augustine of Hippo (354–430), and Leo the Great (c. 390–461). Bishops gather for seventy-five councils during the fourth century, assuming increased responsibility for the Church of the empire as they respond to heresies, reshape church structures, and regulate church life. They also take steps in this century to curb the excesses of deacons, whose control of money and property allows them to take on an exaggerated importance.

Though the ancient diocese might be thought of more like today's extremely large parishes rather than our modern concept of the multi-county diocese of hundreds of thousands of people, the bishop evolves gradually into the supreme authority in his diocese. This growth in responsibility means that the office of bishop becomes more and more administrative, institutional , and semi-monarchical. At the same time, the presbyter's role grows increasingly cultic as the bishop, unable to preside for all of his people at the Sunday Eucharist, dispatches presbyters to outlying areas to preside, sending along on Sundays a fragment of the consecrated bread from the cathedral church as a sign of unity between the bishop and the local church.

This gradual development, coupled with the celebration of the liturgy in basilicas, which naturally emphasizes the ministry of the clergy in the apse (sanctuary), increases the distance between clerics and laity to such an extent that, by the fifth century, clerics are viewed essentially in their cultic role. Bishops and presbyters are both considered priests because, increasingly, they both preside at the Eucharist. Their sacramental role becomes foremost in the popular imagination. It is in this context also that clerical celibacy emerges as a concern.

## ii. The Beginnings of Celibacy

By the time the Council of Elvira in 305 requires that all clergy abstain from being with their wives before assisting at the altar, celibacy begins to become an ideal for presbyters and bishops. In a culture whose dualistic philosophical presuppositions see matter as evil and, therefore, sex as tainted, continence, and later celibacy, come to be seen as necessary for the sake of the cleric's ritual purity. The rise of celibate monasticism creates further pressure. The monastic movement changes the common understanding of holiness. *Apatheia,* passionlessness, becomes the popular spiritual ideal. It demands that the cleric, if he would be authentic in his role, abstain from all that would arouse the passions. It is in the fifth century that the basic categories of monk, cleric, and lay come to the fore; only the monks are celibate at this time. Leadership in a sacrificial worship-oriented religion, however, coupled with civic leadership in a ruined state after the fall of the empire, suggests that clerics need to live a more virtuous, dignified, spiritual, and pure state of life than the laity. The passing of the age of the martyrs and the rise of the monastic ideal leads naturally, albeit with considerable disciplinary imposition over centuries, to the requirement of celibacy for bishops and presbyters.

### E. THE MONASTIC CENTURIES

Monasticism begins as a lay renewal movement when Antony (250–356) flees from the world into the Egyptian desert to return to Christian basics: daily praying the 150 psalms as he weaves baskets, drinking only water, and eating one pound of bread. The movement becomes known widely when Athanasius of Alexandria publishes *The Life of Anthony* in 357. Pachomius (290–346) takes solitary monastic experience and shapes it into community life. Word of Antony and Pachomius brings flocks of people to the Egyptian desert to sit at their feet and follow their example. John Cassian (360–435) travels there in the early fifth century, then brings the story of monasticism to the West when he publishes *The Institutes* and *Conferences,* which describe the life and teachings of the desert monks. Monasticism begins to flourish across the Church, reaching its most enduring form in the West with the *Rule of Benedict,* written by Benedict of Nursia (480–547) between 530 and 540. This monastic rule, complemented by those of Augustine and Basil of Caesarea written a century earlier, becomes the framework for the way of life we come to know as monasticism.

The ministry of the monk is the gospel ideal of praying always, letting nothing be preferred to the *opus Dei,* the work of God. This consists of praying the rounds of the divine office (psalms and Scripture readings), gathering for sacramental liturgy, doing *lectio divina* (sacred reading), and extending hospitality to guests as if to Christ himself. The monasteries assume the ancient deacon role for the Church, caring for the poor and sick, even as they cultivate the land, instruct in agriculture, and become the refuge and custodian for art, literature, and culture. This era begins and ends with monastic popes, Gregory I (590–604) and Gregory VII (1073–1085), both closely associated with Benedictine monasticism. In between these two the monastic movement brings forth 24 popes, more than 200 cardinals, 1,600 bishops, 43 emperors, 44 kings, and 1,560 saints; Europe has more than 1,700 exempt monasteries.[8]

The monastic centuries open with the German Odoacer removing the Emperor Romulus Augustus from his throne in 476.[9] In the competition for control that ensues among the pope, the patriarch of Constantinople, the emperor at Constantinople, and the barbarian Franks, the pope has the independence, strength, and prestige to win. His alliance with the Franks under Pippin, culminating in the crowning of Charlemagne as Holy Roman Emperor at Christmas, 800, forever tips the balance of power in Europe. Meanwhile, to Europe's south, east, and west, Islam expands into Spain toward southern Frankish territory and into the Balkans toward Austria, isolating Europe and turning it inward.

### i. General Church Structure

Diocesan structures are weak during these centuries. The bishops are either feudal princes themselves or struggling against being controlled by feudal princes. Priests in the countryside parishes, unlike those of noble birth ministering in the cities, are generally poorly educated. They focus their work on the sacramental life, providing hope in the midst of dark and dangerous times. Bishops seek out the life of the monasteries to provide renewal for this weak diocesan church, and so the monastic life becomes the ideal for the clergy and sets the tone for the life of the

---

[8] See Bernier, *op. cit.*, 107. Exemption meant that these monastic communities were not subject to the authority of the bishop except with regard to issues of faith and morals, removing from episcopal control the vast lands, income, and resources of the monasteries.

[9] Odoacer deposes the Romulus Augustus, sends the imperial insignia of the West to the emperor at Constantinople, and requests from Zeno that he be formally named *patrician*. Ultimately, Odoacer styles himself *rex*, king. Thus, imperial authority ends in the West. "Odoacer's decision also created a political vacuum in the old capital. Instinctively, men looked for another father figure. And so they raised up the bishop of Rome, already primate of Christendom, investing him with temporal authority as well as spiritual and surrounding him with much of the pomp and semi-mystical ceremonial formerly reserved for the Emperors. The age of the medial papacy had begun." See John Julius Norwich, *A Short History of Byzantium* (New York: Vintage Books, 1997) 54. For further background on the significance of these events see J. B. Bury, *The Invasion of Europe by the Barbarians* (New York: W. W. Norton & Company, 2000) 161–73.

church.[10] The strongest example of monastic influence is perhaps Ireland, where the monasteries overshadow even the hierarchy.[11] It is a time when monastic theology and spirituality reshape the whole Church.

## ii. The Bishop's Role

The role of the bishop increasingly becomes modeled on that of the abbot of a monastery: paternalistic and more concerned about the spiritual life than about coordinating outward-reaching ministries. Monasticism defines the leader of the community in terms of authority and order. This mindset manifests itself in the broader Church through the notion of *jurisdiction*. Proven leadership and spirituality are separated from the right to an office, and so legal authority assumes priority over the charisms of the Spirit and ministry arising from them. As the centuries pass, it becomes a theological presupposition that appointment and ordination to office bring along with them the gifts necessary to exercise office. "We have here the beginning of a great reversal: symbols and legal positions dispensed grace rather than grace begetting life through charisms realized in office and service."[12]

Until these centuries a bishop is considered married to his diocese for life. Gradually, however, bishops begin to move from see to see, elected to broader responsibility by each other rather than by the priests and people of the diocese. The first bishop of Rome to be a bishop before his election to the Roman see, for instance, is Leo III in 795.[13] By the end of the ninth century, the election of men already bishops elsewhere to the See of Peter becomes typical.[14] This pattern gradually extends across the Church, especially for the metropolitan sees.

---

[10] See O'Meara, *op. cit.*, 100, where he notes that these are centuries marked by "(1) economic revival, (2) the fusion of the Latin and Teutonic peoples, (3) the afterlife of Roman Law in the monastic rule, the canon law of the Church, and the Holy Roman Empire, (4) the feudal system, which set up new hierarchies of power and enabled the monastic orders to extend their influence and benefits generally."

[11] For a splendid treatment of this subject, see Thomas Cahill, *How the Irish Saved Civilization: The Untold Story of Ireland's Heroic Role from the Fall of Rome to the Rise of Medieval Europe* (New York: Doubleday, 1995).

[12] O'Meara, *op. cit.*, 102.

[13] This point is not without controversy in that it depends on the definition of the term *cardinal priest*, which seems to refer during this time to bishops who have certain responsibilities at the Lateran basilica. The first pope to have certainly been bishop of another see is Marinus I, elected in 882, who had been bishop of Caere. For centuries prior to this time, most popes had been deacons before election.

[14] After 1059 the College of Cardinals elects the pope.

### iii. *The Shift in the Ideal of Holiness*

The definition of Christian life gradually shifts from being a life of ministry to being an inner life of detachment and contemplation. Consequently, when baptized adults experience deep, inner conversion, they most often enter monastic life. Cathedral schools modeled on the monasteries train men for diocesan ministry, and monastic values shape the candidates. The heart of the experience of the Christian life becomes the cycle of the life of Christ wedded to the cycle of the seasons of the year in the northern hemisphere, expressed ritually through the cycle of the liturgical year. The round of offices prayed in the monasteries becomes idealized as the angelic life. By the eleventh century, this idealization leads to bishops and priests taking on the obligation to pray, even privately, the seven offices of the breviary as the foundation of their personal prayer.

### iv. *Changes in the Mass*

The celebration of Mass during these centuries becomes increasingly inward and withdrawn, focusing more on the presider than the assembly. Language, along with ritual and devotional shifts, plays an important role. When the Franks convert to Christianity, the Roman Mass brought to their lands retains the Latin. Because the language of worship is foreign, the common people and lower clergy reach for understanding and meaning in worship by developing the notion that the Mass is an allegory of the paschal sacrifice of Christ. Formally discouraged by the bishops, but popularly accepted, each element of the eucharistic ritual becomes connected to a moment in the story of Jesus' passion. Furthermore, the Sunday celebration of the Eucharist is increasingly extended to weekday eucharistic commemorations of the *dies natalis* (birth into eternal life) of martyrs and confessors. By the eighth century the Mass, originally and for centuries the pre-eminent celebration of the resurrection of the Lord on Sunday, comes to be celebrated daily.

With more and more priests in monasteries, and an increase in the fervent desire to celebrate the saints and pray for the dead, the Mass gradually comes to be celebrated privately as well. Moreover, with the deepening notion of the sacredness and mystery of the rite, public Mass becomes more and more distant from the people, to the point that the priest is viewed as the only essential participant and presides with his back turned to the assembly. By the ninth century bread is replaced by what we know today as hosts, and soon afterward the cup is withdrawn from the assembly.

*v. Changes in the Understanding of the Ordained*

The understanding of orders also shifts during these centuries. The notion of the cultic priest celebrating the eternal and universal sacrifice of the Mass comes to predominate. The office of priest, then, becomes the paradigm for all other offices in the Church. Episcopal consecration is understood to be an extension of priesthood, a high priesthood. Diaconate comes to be regarded as merely a step toward priesthood. To these offices are added further steps toward priesthood, each more distant from priesthood than the next. These "minor orders," modified after Vatican II in the 1960s but not altogether eliminated, are porter (doorkeeper), lector (reader), acolyte (Mass server), exorcist (spiritual authority), and subdeacon (assistant to the deacon). The investing ritual for each of these seven orders is called "ordination." During the eighth century and afterward, *tonsure* is added as the starting point of the progression. *Tonsure,* a hair-cutting ceremony modeled on the monastic, incardinates (hinges) a candidate into a diocese and guarantees him the rights and privileges of the clerical state. In all of this hierarchical progression, ordination comes to be understood as granting a personal power, which bestows an indelible character, a permanent change in being, upon the ordained.

Celibacy in these centuries, nourished by monastic example and formation, is increasingly urged by Rome. The churches and residences of clergy come more and more to take on the air of cloistered, monastic community life, a way of living that is understood to assist priests with living celibacy faithfully.

Vesture, too, takes on importance. The *pallium,* a strip of lamb's wool decorated with black crosses worn over the shoulders, makes its appearance in the fourth century as a garment worn over street clothes. It emphasizes the dignity of office for Eastern bishops and the bishop of Rome. By the sixth century the bishop of Rome gives the pallium to Western bishops of metropolitan sees as an expression of their union with him. By the ninth century the pallium becomes a symbol of jurisdiction, which metropolitan bishops are required to ask of the pope before they may ordain to holy orders or consecrate a church building.

The *stole,* a long piece of cloth worn around the neck and hanging down from the shoulders, a symbol of office for bishops adopted from the imperial services in the fourth century, gradually becomes a universal, distinguishing badge of office for bishops, priests, and deacons.

The *dalmatic,* originally a floor-length garment of white wool and broad sleeves with purple and red stripes from the shoulders to the floor, originally worn by the Roman noble classes, is first worn by the pope. It is gradually extended honorifically to the deacons of the Roman church until it becomes universally the deacon's ceremonial vestment.

By the ninth century the *chasuble,* a coat-like garment similar to the modern poncho, worn over the dalmatic, becomes the ceremonial presiding vestment for bishops; the chasuble worn without the dalmatic is the presiding vesture for priests. Outside the sanctuary, modest, grave street dress is specified for the clergy.[15]

### vi. By the End of the Monastic Centuries

In summary, beginning with Pope Gregory I sending Augustine of Canterbury to the Anglo-Saxons in the late sixth century, monks are sent to convert barbaric tribes and succeed in doing so. Monasteries, with their Romanesque churches, walled enclosures, shops, scriptoriums, and cultivated fields, emerge as outposts of order and hubs of culture in these converted lands. The bishops, often monks themselves, become both spiritual and temporal rulers. As the papacy increasingly defines itself in feudal and monarchical terms, especially after the gifts of land on the Italian peninsula beginning in 756, the bishops increasingly view themselves as monarchs as well. Holding vast lands and controlling significant revenue apart from the monasteries, all collaborate with and war against each other, motivated by the desire to make Western Europe a perfect society regulated by the will of God, modeled on the monastery.

---

[15] The cassock is mandated by Sixtus V (1585–1590), but his directive was commonly interpreted to mean for ceremonial functions. Black is specified only in the seventeenth century. The collar and cassock at home and in church, and the collar and long coat on the street, are required in the United States at the Third Plenary Council of Baltimore in 1884.

# 4. The Clerical Culture: Set for the Ages

The first thousand or so years of Christianity witnessed the establishment of a culture of clergy separated from the laity. The next thousand years defined and refined the separation, right down to our own day. Though the clerical culture in our time is shaken and fading in many respects, the material, relational, and ideational world that shaped the *clerus* during the last thousand years is alive and well.

## A. THE HARMONY OF HIERARCHY

During the later medieval centuries between the reign of Gregory VII (1073–1085) and the Council of Constance (1414 marks a single pope back on the See of Peter), many elements of church life from the previous centuries are refined and codified. This is an age of great reformers, theologians and canonists: Bernard of Clairvaux (1090–1153) and Bruno (1030–1101) reform monasticism; Dominic (1170–1221), Francis (1182–1226), and Clare (1193–1253) reform religious life by founding the mendicant orders; Catherine of Siena (1347–1380) brings the pope back to Rome from Avignon; great mystics like Bonaventure (1217–1274), Meister Eckhart (1260–1328), and Julian of Norwich (1342–1416) ponder and write about the spiritual life; Albert the Great (1200–1280), Thomas Aquinas (1225–1274), and John Duns Scotus (1300–1361) philosophically ground and make generally systematic the teachings of the Church; Gratian gathers the Church's legal tradition into his *Decretum,* and William Duranti (1230–1296) schematizes and codifies the ordination rituals with all their particulars.[1] Underneath this dazzling

---

[1] Duranti's work, ranking clearly the major and minor orders, establishes the vesture, symbols, and ritual for the ordained until the end of the fifteenth century. Minor revisions are made at that time. These revisions are promulgated by the Council of Trent and remain law until after Vatican II. The impact of Duranti's work during this time period leads, for instance, to the establishment of the colors for the liturgical seasons of the year.

work, the institutional elements of the Church grow organizationally and administratively more complex and more centralized.

### i. The Impact of the Pseudo-Dionysius

The writings of an author whom we today call Pseudo-Dionysius the Areopagite are a pivotal influence that shapes this era.[2] His works gain currency through the *Sentences* of Peter Lombard (1095–1160), studied closely by the clergy during these centuries, and the spiritual works of the canons of St. Victor in Paris.[3] The twefth-century influence of Diony-sius' *The Celestial Hierarchy, The Ecclesiastical Hierarchy,* and *The Divine Names* increases in the thirteenth century and beyond, making a power-ful impact on theology and spirituality. In fact, the Scholastic[4] populari-zation of Dionysius' ideas ultimately means that the notion of hierarchy becomes "the structural model of public and ecclesiastical life."[5] The Scholastics describe the Trinity as the fullness of light and the whole hi-erarchy of being as sharing in this light, with each level in an ascending order. All of reality, then, from rocks to angels, participates in a progres-sive divinization, ending in the beatific vision of God. This understand-ing of reality's structure has far-reaching consequences for the Church.

Because the Scholastic world comes to see the whole of creation as grounded in God and hierarchically ordered, nothing is accidental, noth-ing out of place. *Diakonia,* therefore, no longer defines ecclesial roles, but rather status, dignity, and office define them relative to a divinely or-dained arrangement. This hierarchical mindset perceives that the higher the status of anything or anyone, the greater the perfection. Moreover, within the ecclesiastical hierarchy, this worldview understands the higher offices to contain within them the lower; thus lower offices (and persons) contribute nothing to the higher and more perfect.

---

[2] This author we today know is a sixth-century Syrian. In the Middle Ages he was mis-takenly equated with both Dionysius the Areopagite, a convert of Paul (Acts 17:34), and Denis (d. 258), the first bishop of Paris.

[3] See *Pseudo-Dionysius: The Complete Works,* Classics of Western Spirituality (New York: Paulist Press, 1987) 26–31.

[4] The term *scholastics* is first used as a derogatory term in the sixteenth century. It refers to the system of philosophical and theological thought grounded in Aristotle that begins to arise in the Carolingian Age and is in full force during the thirteenth century at the mo-nastic and cathedral schools and later the universities such as those at Paris, Bologna, Ox-ford, Cambridge, and Toulouse.

[5] Paul Bernier, *Ministry in the Church: A Historical and Pastoral Approach* (Mystic, Conn.: Twenty-Third Publications, 1992) 131.

## ii. The Clerical Hierarchy and the Eucharist

In the life of the Church, the Eucharist is revered as the most perfect manifestation of the divine. Consequently, proximity to the Eucharist defines and gives value to the offices of bishop, priest, deacon, as well as other offices and roles. The relationship between priesthood and the Eucharist, the human touching the Divine as the priest offers the memorial of the supreme sacrifice of the cross, leads the Scholastics to conclude that ordination to priesthood conveys a permanent, indelible character that changes his very being, a change that is, in the teaching of some, eternal.[6] By implication, this makes the priest and bishop "other than" the laity, placing them above lay people.

This hierarchical theology shifts the relationship between priest and bishop. If the Eucharist defines priesthood, and both priest and bishop have the power to say Mass, then what is the difference between the two, the Scholastics ask? When the Fourth Lateran Council in 1215 mandates the yearly confession of sin for all, this change in the sacrament of penance focuses a second formidable sacramental role for the priest: he is now the one to whom people need to go for the forgiveness of their sins. This sacred role increases the priest's sacramental mystique and leads to his being viewed more and more as a moral authority. Both priest and bishop, however, forgive sins. What is the difference between them, the Scholastics ask?

The greater perfection in which the bishop participates—and why a bishop is consecrated and not ordained[7]—comes to be understood in terms of jurisdiction, not sacrament. The bishop has larger governing authority than the priest and can delegate, withhold, restrict, or withdraw his jurisdictional power because of his authority. Jurisdiction is the bishop's greater excellence over the priest. The communal nuances underneath the meaning of ordination in the monastic centuries—a time when society is generally more collegial in its arrangement—changes in the thirteenth century toward understanding ordination in authoritative terms. Ordination becomes the valid transmission of power.

---

[6] The Council of Florence in 1439 first mentions the notion of ontological change conferred by ordination. The Council of Trent reiterates the point in 1563. Florence is also the first affirmation of orders as sacrament. Neither of these councils, however, clarifies the sacramental relationship between bishop and priest. That only comes with Vatican II.

[7] A bishop is not ordained to ministry until after Vatican II, when the order of bishop is first defined as a sacrament in itself and not merely an excellence added onto priesthood.

Priest and bishop have sacramental power by virtue of a character indelibly bestowed at priesthood ordination and by jurisdictional power conferred by proper ecclesiastical authority. These powers are understood to be separate. This separation leads to anomalous practices: priests can be delegated to ordain (e.g., abbots), and laity can exercise ecclesial authority and receive church income without being ordained (e.g., prince bishops).

### iii. Celibacy

Celibacy, in this worldview, is the natural complement to the perfection of the ordained, who are closest to the Eucharist and different in kind over the laity. The largely disciplinary Lateran councils gradually codify celibacy. Lateran I (1123) prohibits clerical marriages, but because the practice continues, Lateran II (1138) makes clerical marriage illegal and invalid. Lateran III (1179) stipulates that, by virtue of his office, the cleric should be provided sufficient income on which to live. Lateran IV (1215) mandates celibacy across the Western Church. Throughout these years, from Pope Gregory VII forward, priests are also highly encouraged to live in community. Though some do, following a monastic model as canons regular in cathedral chapters, living in community proves impractical for many parish priests and generally fails to take hold for diocesan clergy.

During this age of the Gothic cathedrals, priesthood comes to be defined almost exclusively in terms of hierarchical power: the sacramental power to offer the sacrifice of the Mass and absolve sins and the jurisdictional power to assume responsibility over a benefice, receive its income, and govern the Church's life within it according to church law.

The hierarchical perspective, holding nothing accidental or optional, fires the impulse to order all of society according to its principles and legally codify it. The priesthood of the ordained becomes an active priesthood of status and office connected to the Eucharist, not a priesthood of service connected with a particular community of faith. Ordained priesthood exercises carefully prescribed sacramental and jurisdictional power in the Church, and it is dependent on the bishops and on a papacy increasingly preoccupied with its exercise of political power in the Papal States and across Western Europe. The care of souls is reduced to providing sacraments with canonical correctness. The common priesthood of the laity, now understood as a passive priesthood, depends on ordained priests. Ministry becomes, by definition, something done solely by the ordained.

### iv. The Clergy/Laity Split

Firmly planted in the Church's understanding at the end of this era is the notion that all people in the Church fit into one of three categories: clergy, laity, or religious (which means neither clergy nor lay). Whatever good works they might do, the laity are no longer understood to *minister*. Rather, they are ministered unto by the ordained. The language of worship and theology, therefore, as well as the responsibility for Christian service, all regress farther and farther from the laity during these centuries.

### B. PROTESTING REFORM AND COUNTERING IT

During the fourteenth, fifteenth, and early sixteenth centuries, as priests and bishops stand distant from the laity and the papacy falls into decay in its preoccupation with temporal affairs, many grass-root movements arise as an expression of the Church's yearning for a more authentic spirituality and church life.[8] Largely silenced by the Inquisition established by Pope Gregory IX in 1231, these movements represent the desire for reform and are complemented by popular calls for a council here and there during the fifteenth century.

### i. The Questions of the Reformers

By the time Luther nails his theses on the door of the Wittenberg Cathedral in 1517, there are essentially four main issues of concern. One is the relationship between grace and good works, which is obscured by the theological assertion that a bad priest can function sacramentally by virtue of his ordination *ex opere operato* just so long as he intends what the Church intends[9] and that he can function authoritatively so long as he has proper jurisdiction. In response, Reformers seek to reconnect morality

---

[8] These included the Cathars, who believed the world evil and rejected baptism by water and matrimony; the Albigensians, who saw the devil as a rival God, Christ as an angelic spirit, and sacraments as vain practices; the Waldensians, who held the ideal of absolute poverty and rejected the authority of unworthy priests; the Hussites, who believed that moral rectitude was necessary for the exercise of episcopal and papal office; and the Wycliffites, a primitive form of biblical fundamentalists who espoused the vernacular Bible, did not believe in transubstantiation, and stood against unworthy priests exercising authority.

[9] This theological proposition, originally defined by Leo I in the fifth century, comes to ever-greater prominence during ensuing centuries as priests' behavior becomes ever more scandalous.

with office. A second question is justification. If Jesus' sacrifice on Calvary is efficacious once and for all as the Scriptures say, then in what sense is the Mass a sacrifice? More importantly, in what sense does the sacrifice of the Mass continue and bring to completion, as the Church then teaches, the sacrifice of Jesus? Moreover, what is the relationship between grace and good works? Do we achieve salvation, or is it a free gift? What is the place of good works in the Christian life?

A third question is the place of the Scriptures. The Church's centuries-long emphasis is on the tradition, and the teachings and structures that arise within it. The Sacred Scriptures are little read or even known outside theological circles, receiving scant attention beyond their use for proof-texting logical propositions. In response, Reformers seek to ground Christian life in the Scriptures.

A fourth question is the role of the pope, who, in hierarchical thinking, is now understood as the one who holds the essential, most perfect office in the Church, the office from which all the others flow. The evident corruption of popes significantly compromises papal authority in the eyes of Reformers. In addition, the Church's struggle with the state, particularly the Papal States and the Holy Roman Empire in the midst of the rise of nation states across Western Europe, is no small factor in the Reformation. Indeed, ultimately the Western Church splits more because of political than religious factors. Luther, Calvin, Zwingli, and the Reformers struggle with these questions by returning to the Scriptures. They then fashion faith communities in accord with their (sometimes unarticulated) theological presuppositions and with interpretations of the Scriptures adapted to take into account the hard political exigencies—ecclesial and civil—of their particular circumstances.

### ii. The Council of Trent

The Church's response, too late to build bridges for reunion, is the Council of Trent (1545–1547, 1551–1552, and 1562–1563). Viewing the direction taken by the Reformers as a form of disorder, the council fathers desire to express the teachings of the tradition in a clear fashion and to condemn error. The council unifies the Church doctrinally and initiates genuine reform in the centuries that follow. Lacking a theology of Word, and presupposing that the Church's sixteenth-century configuration is of divine origin, Trent seeks not to change but simply to counter reform. Defensive, and likely without full understanding of the theological issues the Reformers raise, the council fails to offer systematic and careful treatment of the Reformers' concerns. Rather, the council fathers focus only on the concerns they believe threatening and therefore necessary to address. Trent offers Catholic theology precious little advance from the Middle Ages.

The council asserts the indelible character of a priesthood ordered to the sacrifice of the Mass over and against the Reformers' tendency to see ministry ordered to preaching and teaching the word. Trent thereby re-iterates the primacy of cult and, at the same time, safeguards sacramental life and the pre-eminence of the clergy. The council understands priesthood ordination as an absolute and independent reality, having no mandatory connection to a particular community of the faithful. The priesthood of the laity is seen as, essentially, a spiritual reality.

The council underscores the need for the priest to have theological competence, spiritual grounding, and sound moral character but re-asserts that the priest's authority rests on ordination alone, whatever the priest's personal gifts and charisms. The hot conciliar issue of jurisdiction leads to the twofold assertion: bishops are superior over priests, and they have a certain independence from the papacy. Regarding authority, the council weights personal power heavier than pastoral service. The centuries-old minor orders, some of which have become obsolete, are reaffirmed as steps to priesthood. The intention of the priest in confecting sacrament, his simply intending to do what the Church does, is given priority over his moral acts.

Trent promulgates certain clerical disciplinary measures. Election to orders means that the cleric has to be ordained within a specified, short period or forfeit income, jurisdiction, and ordination itself. Bishops are required to reside in their dioceses and priests in their parishes, under penalty of law. Following Pope Gregory I's work *Pastoral Care,* the council urges preaching whenever sacraments are celebrated. Trent focuses the responsibility for preaching especially on the diocesan bishop. The council also urges improved formation for the clergy by requiring seminaries in every diocese. That reform, however, which will have significant impact in future centuries, is delayed due to cost.

The Council of Trent takes little note of the religious: monks, brothers, nuns, and friars; it considers the laity only as non-clerics. The passivity of the laity—they would be holy if their priests were holy—is taken for granted. The council's goal is its great accomplishment. It unites the Church.

## C. RAMPARTS CATHOLICISM

The three hundred years from the end of the Council of Trent until the Second Vatican Council (1962–1965) spawn significant architectural, spiritual, organizational, and evangelizing growth and achievement. Baroque and Rococo architecture mark the early centuries, while the Romantic revival architecture of the neo-Romanesque, neo-Gothic, and neo-Classical styles emerges in the nineteenth century. Functional modern architecture appears in the twentieth century. These are also centuries of great spiritual teachers, reformers, founders of religious congregations, and missionaries. Theresa of Avila (1515–1582) and John of the Cross (1542–1591) found the Discalced Carmelites in Spain and write about contemplation. Charles Borromeo (1538–1584) inspires the seminary system. Pierre de Berulle (1575–1629) and Jean-Jacques Olier (1608–1657) found a spiritual school that has a permanent impact on priestly formation, and Olier founds Sainte Sulpice and the Sulpician congregation to staff seminaries. Francis DeSales (1567–1622) writes his *Introduction to the Devout Life* and inspires Jane Frances de Chantal (1572–1641) to leave her family to found the Visitation sisters. Ignatius of Loyola (1491–1556) founds the Jesuits, Philip Neri (1515–1595) the Oratory, and John Baptist De LaSalle (c. 1653–1719) the Brothers of the Christian Schools. Vincent De Paul (1581–1660) works to reform the French clergy, establishes a congregation focused into seminary education, the Vincentians, and, with Louise de Merillac (1591–1660), founds the Daughters of Charity. The Franciscans and Jesuits bring the Gospel to the Americas, India, China, and Japan. As dioceses are established in mission lands, the founding missioners are followed by ancient and new religious orders of women and men who establish parishes, schools, hospitals, orphanages, and centers of learning. In the nineteenth century Jean Marie Vianney (1786–1859) lives out his holiness in the parish at Ars, and Thérèse of Lisieux (1873–1897) lives out hers in a Carmelite convent. In the twentieth century Frances Xavier Cabrini (1850–1917) travels the oceans ministering to the immigrants of the Americas, and Maximillian Kolbe (1894–1941) gives his life for another at Auschwitz.

### i. The Church Turned Inward

In the midst of the enormous missionary and educational outreach of these centuries, the Church paradoxically remains essentially turned inward. Characterized by Tridentine defensiveness and increasing Roman centralization, for two centuries the Catholic Church sees the enemy not as the scientific rationalism that flourishes and reshapes Western society but as Protestantism. When Rome finally reacts to the intellectual movements of the time, it condemns three hundred years of modernity in the Syllabus of Errors of 1864, reluctantly blesses the labor movement with Pope Leo XIII's encyclical *Rerum novarum* in 1891, and, during the reign of Pope Pius X, digs in against the emerging modern consciousness manifest in historical, archeological, and scriptural studies. Meanwhile the Church loses from its membership, or from religious practice, much of the working class in Europe, many men in Latin cultures, and much of the scientific rationalist intelligentsia across the world.

## ii. The Ordained

After Trent, the theological focus on the Mass as sacrifice continues to require a priesthood focused on cult. Insistence on the performance of correct ritual leads to relatively mechanical celebration together with the tendency to objectify sacraments. Such objectification, coupled with the notion of the indelible sacramental character of orders, de-emphasizes both God's and the Church's action in sacrament as well as the assembly's participation. This movement not only underscores strongly the person of the priest, it exalts the very notion of priesthood itself.

Because of the invigoration of priesthood formation through the seminary system, priests come to their role better prepared and with greater integrity than in the past. They continue to be understood, however, as cultic figures whose role is to celebrate Mass and help form Christ in others through spiritual direction. The purpose of the priest is to say Mass, absolve sins, and thus save souls. Centuries of trends are now cemented in place by seminary formation.

The spirituality of the clergy, renewed through the teaching and writing of Berulle, Olier, and Ignatius Loyola, is spread through seminary faculties instructed in the principles of the French School and formed by the *Spiritual Exercises* of Ignatius. The ideal of self-denial manifest in the Crucified is held up for all Christians but especially for the priest. Meditating on the human life of Jesus, particularly his passion, re-enacted and continued in the sacrifice of the Mass, helps nurture personal virtue and personal relationship with Jesus Christ. It focuses on the individual, the personal, and the experiential, however, rather than the communal. For the whole of the Church this trend grows as eucharistic devotions outside Mass, like Forty Hours and Benediction, as well as devotions to the Sacred Heart of Jesus or the Virgin Mary, multiply during this age. By the time Pope Pius XI in 1929 offers St. John Marie Vianney to the world as

patron of diocesan priests, rigorous personal discipline, along with life focused on Mass and the ministry of the confessional, become the ideal of
the priest.

The bishop's role shifts during these centuries as well. The idealization of the Society of Jesus and the Jesuit role in the education of clergy
shift the model of relationship between bishop and priests. Rather than
being the coordinator of ministries in his diocese, or abbot-like spiritual
father, the bishop becomes like the Jesuit superior: personally responsible
for priests' welfare, inquiring about their spiritual life and expecting an
obedience in which the priest receives the bishop's word as a morally
obliging manifestation of the will of God. This shift marks the final
movement toward the bishop being understood as a kind of monarch in
his diocese.

### iii. Increasing Centralization of the Church

As the papacy grows stronger, canonizing the monarchical with the
declaration of infallibility at Vatican I, the pope increasingly becomes
understood as the supreme and immediate pastor of the Church universal, with the bishop as his local delegate. Centralization toward the papacy leads to an idealizing of the pope and the expansion of the Vatican
curia. It also leads to a system of papal ambassadors, nuncios, and apostolic delegates, who not only spread across the world to represent the
Vatican to civil governments but also to oversee the ecclesial life of national hierarchies. Monarchical control takes such ineluctable hold in
the Church that local pastors come to be perceived as delegates of the
bishop and expect their word to be accepted with religious obedience by
parishioners. Pastors feel duty bound to regulate parish life tightly, exercising their ministry with both a keen sense of accountability to the
bishop as well as a differentiated sense of their right to appeal over the
bishop's head under certain circumstances.

In contrast, these centuries see the massive rise of religious congregations taking up particular ministries in the Church, from mission
work to education to health care. Women religious are in the vanguard
of this movement, doing heroic ministry across the globe, sharing in
what the Church officially calls the "apostolate of the hierarchy."[10] Both
women and men religious begin to associate lay people with this ministry in the eighteenth century through the founding of fraternities and
sodalities. This leads to the development of Catholic Action in the nine-

---

[10] See Paul Bernier, *op. cit.*, 200, quoting Pope Pius XI.

teenth century. These lay groups largely focus their efforts toward ordering the worlds of politics and labor. They begin to animate ministry for some laity, but the laity remain unable to touch anything in the Church's institutional structure or ritual. They evangelize only as a by-product of their Catholic Action. The masses of laity remain in their parishes sitting passively in the pew.

## D. THE SECOND VATICAN COUNCIL

Pope John XXIII surprises the world when he calls Vatican II. It is a time of calm. In response to his call, controversy swirls around the advisability of a council. Nonetheless it begins in 1962.

Because of the largely anti-intellectual stand in many Vatican documents over the previous century, and the narrow defensiveness of both seminary formation and the Vatican curia, much of the history reviewed so far is little understood by many of the council fathers. Moreover, conflicting points of view find their way into the council's documents as committees write them for near-unanimous council approval. Still, as the council throws open the windows of the Church, expert theological argument wins the day and Vatican II brings monumental shifts of understanding regarding clerics, changes we have yet to fully comprehend, let alone accept or implement.

The Dogmatic Constitution on the Church, commonly called *Lumen gentium,* refrains from closely defining the Church but rather calls it a mystery grounded in God. The essence of this mystery is communion: profound spiritual relationship with God and one another in the Church. Baptism and confirmation initiate communion relationship and Eucharist nurtures it, proclaiming the universal call to holiness for all in the Church. All have a vocation, a call, sustained by the Holy Spirit, to continue the priestly, prophetic, and kingly ministry of Jesus Christ in the world. While sacraments and ministries shape the Church, the Holy Spirit's charismatic gifts are to be honored and used by all for the sake of building up the common good so the world may ever more resemble the dominion of the Kingdom of God.

Vatican II's Pastoral Constitution on the Church in the Modern World, commonly called *Gaudium et spes,* calls for reshaping the relationship between the Church and the world. The Church exists for the world, it says, and serves the world. The ideal is no longer flight from the world and saving one's soul but moving out to the world, with all Christians, not merely the ordained, on mission to the world and within it. The Church is no longer understood to be a perfect society, itself the kingdom. Rather, the Church is a pilgrim people striving to serve the Kingdom of God. While the document tends to focus priests toward the Church and laity toward the world, it clearly calls for all Christians to collaborate together in serving the Kingdom by striving to transform the world.

### i. Redefinition of Roles Lay and Ordained

While the council documents generally understand the laity to have the role of harmonizing work and culture toward moral values, the laity have the right and duty to express their opinions in the ordering of the Church as well. The hierarchical principle is de-emphasized; states of life in the Church are no longer viewed as higher or lower. All Christians pursue perfection as they follow their call; women and men are valued equally as living instruments of the mission of the Church.

The bishop's role is significantly reshaped as well. He is no longer understood to be empowered by the pope for his ministry, as if he were some kind of branch manager. Rather, the bishop is pastor of the local church in his own right. He is not a priest with greater jurisdiction. Rather, the office of bishop, not that of the priest, is understood as the primary office in the Church. Episcopacy is, itself, the fullness of priesthood through which all other offices need to be understood. Ordination is viewed as a work of God enacted through sacrament, and ordination to the episcopacy is, for the first time in church history, acknowledged as a sacrament in itself. The bishops as a group, then, are teachers, sanctifiers, and leaders of the Church in a collegial way. Their decisions, made in consultation with the bishops of other local churches, give their ministry its apostolic dimension, which is grounded in the constellation of relationships they enjoy in the universal college of bishops. Their hierarchical ministry is viewed in pastoral, rather than in exclusively juridical, terms. They are no longer like abbots or religious superiors to presbyters, but charged to live in a fraternal relationship with them.

Presbyters[11] in the Church, both in *Lumen gentium* and The Decree on the Ministry and Life of Presbyters, called *Presbyterium ordinis,* come to be understood not as delegates of the bishop, but as co-workers. Presbyters

---

[11] See ibid., 223. Bernier notes here that the first title given to the document on priests was entitled "On clerics," then the title changed to "On priests," then to "On the life and ministry of priests," then, finally, to "On the ministry and life of Presbyters." This evolution is remarkable in that the shift is from state of life to pastoral role, from offering sacrifice to pastoral leadership, and by implication, from absolute ordination to ordination into a college of presbyters within a particular local church.

are ordained by an act of God, through the agency of the bishop, to publicly serve the Church by fostering community. Presbyters are not ministers of the Church but ministers of Christ for the sake of the Church. They minister neither in the name of the bishop nor representing the bishop but under the bishop's authority, in the person of Christ. Their ministry has an apostolic quality because, in the context of the local church's presbyteral college, the presbyter's role calls him to advise the bishop regarding the local church out of their experience of teaching, sanctifying, and leading. Preaching and teaching are essential to their sacramental role, not merely a nicety. Presbyters are also invited to acknowledge and foster the humble and exalted charisms of the laity so they might play their own active role in the Church and in the world.

The ordained bishop and presbyter are still understood by the council to be essentially different from the laity, but Vatican II documents refrain from the "indelible character" theology. Rather, they open to understanding the essential difference between priests and laity as the constellation of relationships, and the shape of those relationships, brought about by ordination. The public nature of presbyteral ministry, its commission to be co-worker with the bishop by maintaining and fostering community, and its ministering within the college of the local church's presbytery—these elements give presbyters their unique place in the Church.

### ii. Trent and Vatican II

Vatican II represents a major correction to the trends of more than a millennium and one-half ensconced by the Council of Trent. The correction might be summarized in this way:[12] Trent's point of departure for understanding priesthood is the Eucharist; Vatican II begins with the mission of the whole Church. Trent understands the priesthood to have been instituted at the Last Supper. Vatican II sees priesthood as emerging from the whole of Jesus' apostolate across his public ministry. The defining element of priesthood for Trent is mystical power over the eucharistic body of Jesus Christ. The defining element for Vatican II is pastoral responsibility over the body of Christ that is the Church. The content of priestly ministry is cult for Trent; it is the mission of the Church for Vatican II. The priest is to find God through worship for Trent. For Vatican II, the presbyter is to find God through faithfulness to the Church's mission. Trent understands the primary ordained ministry

---

[12] See ibid., 231.

to be that of priest, with that of bishop being a consecration of a priest, an added excellence having to do with jurisdiction.

Vatican II understands the primary ordained ministry to be that of bishop, now understood, for the first time, to be a sacrament in its own right. It understands presbyters, in the college of the local church, to be co-workers of the bishop in preaching, teaching, and presiding at sacrament as well as in pastoral leadership. Trent sees priesthood ordination as bestowing an indelible character, a change in being rendering the priest ontologically different from the laity. Vatican II sees ordination as making the bishop or presbyter essentially different because of his constellation of relationships: public pastoral leadership in the local church, collegial ministry with peers, and the resulting constellation of relationships within the Church.

Vatican II represents a remarkable return to the apostolic origins of ministry in the Church. Contrary to centuries of trends, it also opens up the Church to the vast expansion of ministry. Within these enormous changes we are still finding our way.

## E. THE MEANING OF *CLERICAL CULTURE* TODAY

We are living in a time of massive transition in the Church. It behooves us to know our history, name our demons—even in the midst of controversy—and grope together toward attitudes and actions that will shape well our future. These tasks are difficult in our time, however. Understanding centuries of ministerial contraction into cultic priesthood, the enshrining of this trend by Trent, then its deepening by the spirituality that emerges in France during the seventeenth and eighteenth centuries, helps clarify why the clerical culture became the bulwark it is in the life of the Church. Throughout every age and time, clerics have had qualities admirable and ignominious. How they have lived has inspired and scandalized. As the Church journeyed through the centuries, however, we hardly even knew that the trajectory was toward contraction of ministry. The Church simply responded to the age, as it does in every age and as it is doing now.

Vatican II made a profoundly significant shift. It expanded ministry, the implications of which are still evolving in our age. Significant questions remain open: What are the ministry structures in the Church? Which ministries are recognized and which not? Is the people's right to the Eucharist to be given real priority? Can we come to consensus about a truly coherent spirituality of ordained ministry for the bishop, presbyter, and deacon? Other open questions, though not without controversy, are the discipline of celibacy, the status of women, the ordination of women, a balanced theology of the presbyter who is a professed religious and the appointment of bishops. We are only in the early stages of addressing these concerns.

The immense and unwieldy weight of our history presses upon us. Very many of the attitudes and ways of life to which our history led remain among bishops and presbyters. The enormous import of Vatican II and the way of life it calls forth continue to be pondered. Our still-uninformed, halting, and contentious comprehension of what was, coupled with some considerable confusion and lack of consensus about what might be, combine to explain why we are living in such a tense and conflicted age. The clerical culture that was is stoutly defended, and even the object of longing among some. It is disdained and vigorously opposed by others. However one judges its current shape, it is lived by bishops and presbyters every day—knowingly and unknowingly—even as it is publicly falling apart.

The history above intimates layers upon layers of meaning underneath the word *clerical* and the term *clerical culture*. Our own age adds layers even as it shifts others. In this context clerical culture refers to the trajectory of material reality, relationship structures, and universe of ideas that, across the centuries, have come to characterize the world of the ordained in the Latin Rite of the Western Dispensation of the Roman Catholic Church. The word *clerical* refers to the ordained person who is formed and who serves the Roman Catholic Church in the trajectory of this culture.

# 5. Theological Underpinnings

Because the orders of bishop, priest, and deacon have theological underpinnings, so does the clerical culture. In *The Changing Face of the Priesthood* Donald Cozzens writes about the "cultic model of priesthood."[1] In this understanding of priesthood, Cozzens writes, the priest fulfills his role above all in the sacred liturgy as "mediator between God and human beings; the provider of the sacraments; the guardian of sacred space and sacred truth."[2] This summary is only somewhat apt. Greater nuance is most helpful.

## A. DULLES' MODELS: A HANDLE FOR UNDERSTANDING

Theologian Avery Dulles, s.j., offers a handy rubric for understanding the Church and its ministries through his use of models. While the five models he offers are never experienced discretely in the Church, and no one of them can be experienced in pure form, they offer a helpful framework for reflecting on various understandings of the clergy and, therefore, clerical culture.[3]

Dulles' *institutional model* of Church is best understood by analogy to the secular state. The institutional model considers the Church to be a perfect society in which the ordained minister is a member of a caste of ruling elite with legally defined powers. These powers are traditionally stated as those of teaching, governing, and sanctifying. While bishop, priest, and deacon all teach, essentially the priest and bishop sanctify and govern. The governing role of bishop, far greater than that of the priest, is also hierarchically stratified. A bishop might be the auxiliary of a dio-

---

[1] Donald B. Cozzens, *The Changing Face of the Priesthood* (Collegeville: The Liturgical Press, 2000) 5.

[2] Ibid.

[3] Avery Dulles, s.j., *Models of the Church: Expanded Edition* (New York: Doubleday Image Books, 1987). See especially 161–75.

cese, who has delegated governing power, and he may be the pope, who has supreme and immediate governing power over the universal Church.

Because, according to this model, power is ultimately derived from God, its exercise is commanding for any who hierarchically have less power than the one exercising it. The faithful, of course, though they have defined rights and duties, have the least power of all. This model offers compelling clarity and order. It can, however, obscure the spiritual mission of the Church and distance it from the mystery of Jesus Christ. Though elements of this model appear in all the Churches, it is particularly Catholic. The model is born in the reign of Constantine, fully articulated by the Scholastics, and set for the ages by the Council of Trent.

The second model is that of the Church as a *mystical communion* of believers bound by the gifts of the Holy Spirit. This ecclesiology stresses the Church's immediate relationship to God, the communion of the individual with the Church, and within the Church, with God. This model aims ministry toward the fostering of fellowship through which the Church grows and is nurtured as a living community of faith on pilgrimage toward the kingdom. The ordained are viewed essentially as leaders of communities, like conductors of an orchestra. The effectiveness of the role of bishop, priest, and deacon rests more in their charism for leading and animating the community of believers than in ordination itself.

Mystical communion ecclesiology, which finds its roots in the epistles of Paul, rose to the fore in the twentieth century and took center stage in the 1940s with Pius XII's encyclical *Mystici Corporis*. It dramatically became front and center during the Second Vatican Council in the *Lumen gentium* (The Dogmatic Constitution on the Church) image of the pilgrim people of God. Both of these images, the somewhat vertical one of the Church as the Body of Christ "head and members" and the horizontal one of the Church as the pilgrim people of God, are variations within this ecclesiology. The model underlines servant leadership in community. It obscures, however, the sacramental dimensions of church life. The overall feel of this model brings to mind especially the Christian churches of the first generation through the third century.

The third model of the Church is the *sacramental,* in which the ordained minister acts as ritual leader, sacred mediator for the sake of the people and on their behalf. The high priesthood theology that begins to surface in the third century, with the bishop considered to be the one who sacrifices on the people's behalf, finds its home in this model. In the sacrament model, the ordained minister brings about the presence of God, and so is a sign of God's presence in the community. Ordination gifts the ordained with the Holy Spirit, setting deacon, priest, and bishop aside for sacred service. It implicitly calls them to holiness, withdrawal from the world, prayer, and penance. This model leads to a high spirituality among the ordained and grounds celibacy. It can obscure the humanity of the ordained, however, by setting them apart in garb and living, exalting them as "other than" the faithful, and focusing their ministry such that they, and only they, are considered as, indispensably, Church. This model can too readily divide the sacred from the profane, leaving the laity out in the world feeling distant from the holy, from being Church.

The fourth model is that of the Church as *herald,* with the dominant emphasis being proclamation of the Word. Following from the preached Word, ritual in this model is but an extension of the Word. It is the presence of God in the Word that brings holiness to a profane world, bearing the power of grace and transformation. This model, emphasized by the Protestant Reformers, affirms the real power of any Christian who would proclaim the Word through preaching, teaching, and witness. It can obscure the efficacy of sacrament and the integral ecclesial ministry of community building.

The Church as *servant* to the world is the fifth model of ecclesiology Dulles offers. Ordained ministry, and the essential ecclesial ministry, turns out to the world to transform it in peace and justice. This model, come to life in Catholicism during the mid-twentieth century, invites the ordained to see their role as calling all in the Church to reflect on the whole array of their life responsibilities in light of the Gospel and shape the social and political order according to gospel values. Affirming the complete unity of sacred and profane, this model can obscure the sacramental in church life and risk embroiling the Church too deeply in particular social or political concerns.

Throughout the centuries the Christian Churches have witnessed to the varied understandings of ministry among the ordained and the laity. The needs of a particular place and time shape how ministry is exercised, and the various models leave wide berth for the possibilities. Yet it must be argued that all of these possibilities, in healthy tension with one another, must be exercised by the priests of any age or place in such a way that the emphasis of each is honored in the whole experience that is Church.

## B. *COMMUNIO* THEOLOGY

Having reviewed Dulles' models, it is a temptation to assume that the cultic model of priesthood to which Cozzens refers arises out of a blending of the institutional and sacramental models of Church. It is a further temptation to suggest that the less happy elements of the clerical culture arise from this same blend. Indeed, these two ecclesiological models easily carry the freight that the purpose of the ordained is to teach, govern, and sanctify; therefore, they are an educated, ruling, and cultic elite. These assumptions, however, are something of a caricature. They take us only a short distance toward insight. A comparison of differing *communio* ecclesiologies, on the other hand, might help us understand more clearly the theological issues that underpin especially the more unfortunate elements of clerical culture. To illustrate the point, I will very briefly compare two *communio* ecclesiologies: one Cardinal Joseph Ratzinger's, the other, Cardinal Avery Dulles'.[4]

### i. Ratzinger and Dulles Compared

Both Ratzinger and Dulles see *communio* ecclesiology as the framework that best integrates most of the current understandings of Church. Ratzinger emphasizes the Church as mystical body of Christ.[5] As noted above, this rather vertical image refers to the Church as the body of Christ "head and members" or the body of Christ "conformed to Christ the head." The hierarchical, and therefore the institutional, inheres within this *communio* ecclesiology. Moreover it is noteworthy, and was a source of some consternation, that the 1985 Extra-ordinary Synod celebrating Vatican II hallowed *communio* ecclesiology even as the dominant council image "people of God" was avoided.[6] This more horizontal image

---

[4] This material largely comes from Michael Papesh, *Ministry in God's Image: A Trinitarian Model of Collaboration for the Parish*, doctoral thesis (1990).

[5] The Ratzinger material is scattered throughout his work. The bulk of it comes from two sources: Joseph Ratzinger, *Principles of Catholic Theology: Building Stones for a Fundamental Theology* (San Francisco: Ignatius Press, 1987) and his *Feast of Faith* (San Francisco: Ignatius Press, 1981).

[6] Controversy swirled at the time of the synod because of recent publication of the Vittorio Messori interview of Cardinal Ratzinger published as Joseph Ratzinger, *The Ratzinger Report*, with Vittorio Messori (San Francisco: Ignatius Press, 1985), which was critical of developments after the council. Also see *Final Report, Origins* (vol. 15, no. 27, December 19, 1985) (Washington D.C.: National Catholic News Service) 446, 448. Also see Peter Hebblethwaite, "Exit 'the people of God,'" *The Tablet* (vol. 240, no. 7596, February 2, 1986) 140–41.

of the Church was a source of inspiration and hope for many in the council's wake. The more vertical mystical body image served better the agenda of those who controlled the synod, including Cardinal Ratzinger.

Avery Dulles, s.j., develops in his work a *communio* ecclesiology that uses an image emphasizing neither the horizontal nor the vertical, but including both: the Church as Community of Disciples.[7] The differences between Ratzinger's more hierarchical and Dulles' more moderate *communio* ecclesiology are significant. For our purposes, I would note four.

First, each emphasizes different elements of what it is to be Church. Ratzinger's ecclesiology comes "from above." He understands the Church, Christ's Body head and members, as the sacrament of God's presence in the world. Dulles' ecclesiology comes "from below." He understands the Church, at the feet of the Lord and sent forth from his side, as the sacrament of humanity before God. For Ratzinger, leaning heavily toward a sacramental subtext in his *communio* ecclesiology, the Church is essentially other than the world. For Dulles, integrating both servant and herald ecclesiological themes in his *communio* ecclesiology, the Church is both one with the world and a contrast community that serves as a transforming community, a leaven, in the midst of the world.

Second, each sees the effects of baptism differently. For Ratzinger, baptism brings the human person into communion with the Trinity, into the "indestructible aliveness of God."[8] Baptism initiates the enlightened into "sonship" with God, and incorporates the human person into the Body of Christ. Ratzinger describes sonship as prayerful communion with God,[9] a sitting at Jesus' feet to hear the word of God and respond to it in prayer. Dulles emphasizes again his desire to integrate the servant and herald models of ecclesiology as he characterizes baptism. He describes baptism as initiating the Christian into the community of disciples to sit at the Master's feet in fellowship and prayer and, further, commissioning the Christian to evangelize, to go forth from the Master's side to preach and teach, to serve and to imitate Jesus in all we say and do.

---

[7] The Dulles material shows development in Dulles' thinking, leading him to settle on the Church as a community of disciples as the most integrating of ecclesiological models. The development of his thought begins in Avery Dulles, s.j., *Models of the Church* (Garden City, N.Y.: Image books, 1978) and its expanded edition (1987). It extends in Avery Dulles, s.j., *A Church to Believe In: Discipleship and the Dynamics of Freedom* (New York: Crossroad, 1982).

[8] Ratzinger, *Principles*, 32.

[9] Ibid., 32. Also see Ratzinger, *Feast of Faith*, 25–32, for a full exposition of Ratzinger's understanding of prayer in relationship to the Trinity.

Third, each sees holy orders differently. Holy orders admits one to what Ratzinger calls "apostleship." Emphasizing the institutional and sacramental, Ratzinger holds that the ordained serve in a role of authority that mediates between the Church and the Father. The ordained are the ministers of communion, holiness, universality, and continuity because the concrete form that the identity of the Church takes in history, as the sacramental *communio,* is apostolic succession. Apostolic succession, priestly office, is, for Ratzinger, the structure that is "the expression both of the link with tradition and of the concept of tradition in the catholic Church."[10] This ministry—the pope in the college of bishops, the bishop in the college of presbyters—represents Christ, proclaims the word and transmits the ministry of apostleship to others.

Dulles' understanding of holy orders notes the institutional and sacramental elements, but more lightly, even as it integrates the herald and servant models of ecclesiology. Holy orders is what Dulles calls an "intensification of discipleship."[11] It is a ministry of leadership, authority, and service given to those who have public charge of communities and the public authority to preach and to preside at worship. For Dulles, the ordained are those within the community of disciples who commit their whole lives to leadership.

Note well here the crucial differences. The fundamental category for ministry in Ratzinger's theology is holy orders. Taking a posture rooted in the Constantinian age and solidified in the Scholastic era, Ratzinger holds that holy orders commissions the ordained to ministry. Planted firmly in the theology of the first three centuries, Dulles sees baptism as the fundamental category for ministry. Baptism commissions all to ministry.

Fourth, Ratzinger and Dulles are consistent with their theology of holy orders in their descriptions of the role of the laity in the Church. For Ratzinger, the role of the laity is to give their lives over to communion with God in prayer and to help make the world around them holy. For Dulles, the role of the laity is to preach, teach, offer service, and imitate Jesus Christ so as to transform the world.

In summary, Ratzinger has a relatively inward understanding of Church and a powerful but somewhat passive notion of baptism's effects. Ratzinger sees hierarchy as a "service to the baptized,"[12] yet he casts the role of the ordained as the only ones in the Church who bear

---

[10] Ratzinger, *Principles,* 245.

[11] Dulles, *ACBI,* 12.

[12] Ratzinger, *The Ratzinger Report,* 49.

authority. They are mediators between God and the community whose ministry is focused within the Church, not to the world. When Ratzinger claims that apostolic succession is the concrete form that the identity of the Church takes in history, that "believing individuals become community only when they exist in the context of the ministry of *successio*,"[13] one can get the impression that the ordained are somehow more the Church than the baptized. Consequently, Ratzinger's theology—integrating the institutional and sacramental understandings of Church and ministry with the *communio*, and firmly planted in the historical development of the Church post-Constantine—seems to risk legitimating the more problematic notes of clerical culture: elitist and sacral culture, inwardness, exclusivity, dependency, privilege, and moral double standards between lay and ordained.

Dulles, on the other hand, offers us a helpful direction with a theology that undercuts these more problematic elements of clerical culture. Dulles hearkens back to the pre-Constantinian centuries, integrating the herald and servant models of ecclesiology and ministry while de-emphasizing the institutional model especially. He offers an expansive view of the Church as a transformation community that is both a sacrament of humanity and a leaven to transform the world. He sees baptism as both our initiation into a lifetime of mystagogy and our being commissioned to go forth to preach, teach, serve, and model Jesus Christ. He closely identifies ordained and lay in the single community of disciples, distinguishing them only in that discipleship is intensified for the ordained, who give their lives to leadership. For Dulles, the Church is all of us together sitting at the Lord's feet, and all of us sent forth to proclaim the Good News, each of us having respective roles to play, all of us sharing *communio* with God and one another. Dulles' theological perspective calls into question the more problematic elements of the clerical culture, and even stands against them.

### ii. Implications for Transforming Clerical Culture

Both *communio* theological perspectives are rich. Both have their problems. With regard to clerical culture, however, Ratzinger's theology buttresses its more problematic elements while Dulles provides a helpful framework for cultural change. The lesson to be learned is twofold. First, transformation of the clerical culture requires us to reach back to the the-

---

[13] Ratzinger, *Principles,* 296.

ology of Church and ministry found in the first three centuries in order to better understand and live out more authentically Gospel teaching. Without denying the legitimate developments of history, it is critically important to be discerning about the directions those developments have taken the Church in relationship to the teachings of Jesus Christ and the New Testament. The accommodations the Church has made to the ages are not to be hallowed uniformly. Second, transformation of the clerical culture requires that we develop a theology of Church and ministry that honors the institutional but, more importantly, integrates community building, worship, preaching, and transforming service of the world as the call of the whole Church, ordained and lay, modeled on the ministry of Jesus Christ.

## C. THEOLOGY OF GOD

Another theological concern critical to the underpinnings of clerical culture and the possibilities for changing it is underneath our understanding of Church and ministry. It is our understanding of God, who is a Trinity of persons absolutely one in love yet distinct in mission. As the Christian dogma that distinguishes us among the world's monotheistic religions, Trinity is the primary and indispensable reality against which the Church needs to assess our life together. Since the Western Church's traditional emphases in the theology of God, evident in both its teaching and its prayer, are a vast subject far beyond the scope of this reflection, I would make a couple of observations to provoke thought.

First, recall the images of the Trinity that depict an ancient man with a white beard in a papal tiara bent over the crucified on the cross, while the Holy Spirit, in the form of a dove, hovers. This image, for all of the Father's compassion in it, relies on papal and monarchical imagery. It proclaims hierarchy in God. It is also somewhat stunted in that it proclaims the centrality of the death of Jesus without note of Jesus' resurrection. Furthermore, the image raises proportion questions about the role of the Spirit, a little dove hovering over the very large action of Father and Son, who are the center of attention.

By comparison, consider the image of the Trinity offered in the Rublev icon that comes to us from the Eastern Church (Russia):[14] three persons seated around a common table, all with the same aspect, each distinctly garbed. All three persons around the table are equally holy, royal, otherworldly, and celestial. All are neither male nor female. Yet

---

[14] See the dedication page above for a black and white reproduction of the Rublev image.

each person is distinct in a way that complements and accents the unity of the three rather than detracts from it. In this image we see three absolutely equal yet distinct persons seated at table, sharing hospitality around the cup of the new covenant in Christ's blood.

The implications of these very different images are worth our pondering. Any theology that would tend to image God in a way that implies hierarchy in God is inaccurate. In relationship to clerical culture, such a theology leads us in an untoward direction. Absolute communion in love and distinctness in one common mission is who God is. Our God models for us who we are and need to be as Church: lay and ordained together, absolutely one in one common mission, each exercising distinct roles in the Church and the world in such a way that we complement and accent our unity rather than detract from it.

Second, a concern we need to consider much more deeply in the Western Church is our theology of the Holy Spirit. We in the West are clear about the role of the God the Father in creation and redemption and are intensely focused on the role of the Son in creation and redemption and in the Church, the extension of Christ's body, head and members, throughout the world. However, we considerably underplay the role of the Holy Spirit. This is evident in the first image of Trinity cited above. It is most clearly evident in how we pray.

Our liturgical orations invoke the Holy Spirit only at the beginning of the Eucharist, and then only in the first option for our prayer. Most other orations in Eucharist, the vast majority, address God the Father through the mediation of Christ our Lord, failing to even mention the Holy Spirit. The traditional moment of transformation within Eucharist for the East is the epiclesis, when the priest extends his hands over the bread and wine and invokes the Holy Spirit. In the West it is the institution narrative, the words of Jesus. We in the West fail in our prayer, and therefore in our believing, to hold the Holy Spirit in his equal position to the Father and the Son.

How would we understand the Church, and everyone's respective role within it, if we gave rightful, wide berth in our ecclesial life to the wind and fire of the Holy Spirit? What would clerical culture look like if we held, in a different balance than we do, the institutional and the charismatic elements of the Church?[15] What is the impact on us in the

---

[15] Dulles, *ACBI*, 29–40, for a full treatment of his view on the institutional and the charismatic elements of the Church and the kind of balance between them he thinks needs to be struck.

West that the Holy Spirit is the runt person of the Trinity in our theology and our prayer?

## D. CONCLUSION

The theological concerns raised above may seem like distinguishing angels on pinheads to some, yet we need to study, ponder, and pray about them most closely and carefully. Why? Even leaving plenty of room for personal inconsistency, our fundamental theological assumptions shape how we think and what we say and do as Church. Our operating theology shapes how we choose to live within or accept clerical culture. If we tend to be too inward, exclusive, and dependent upon the institution, if we are content to have among us a privileged caste, somewhat aloof and living a moral double standard, then we are making particular public theological statements about the identity and purpose of God, the Church, baptism, orders, ordained, and lay. The same is true, of course, if we are, all of us together in the Church, lay and ordained, outward moving, expansive and independent in a healthy way, presenting ourselves humbly and simply, compassionately identifying with all people, living and insisting upon a single moral standard across all our relationships.

Every Catholic in the United States, ordained and lay, individually and corporately in our communities, needs to critically reflect on his or her operating theology, what it is and what he or she wants it to be. Our Christian life makes theological statements about what we value and believe. Our theology, in turn, shapes our Christian life together: its universe of ideas, its relationship structures, and its material reality.

# Part Two:
# The Contradictions

# 6. Priestly Formation

## A. SEMINARY FORMATION

The word *seminary* comes from the Latin word for seed. A *seminarium* is a seedbed, the place where seedlings are prepared for eventual planting in the garden, field, or vineyard. The place for priestly formation came to be known as *seminary* with its increased institutionalization in the sixteenth century after the Council of Trent. Trent made it obligatory for each diocese across the world to have a seminary, recommending that it be built near the cathedral of the diocese so that the seminarian might serve his apprenticeship there, pray with the community of *canons*,[1] and serve the bishop. Trent also permitted dioceses to join together to establish a common seminary for a group of dioceses. Thus, seminaries for clergy formation evolved into what we today know them to be after the Council of Trent and in response to the Protestant Reformation.

### i. Some Historical Perspective

The formation of the clergy has always been and remains today a chief responsibility of the bishop. For this reason, from the earliest times men who wished to become priests gathered around the bishop to learn theology and pastoral practice. Relatively informal for centuries, this process of pastoral leadership formation led to an uneven preparation of clergy from diocese to diocese.

In response to uneven formation, the papacy directed in the early ninth century that schools be established near the cathedral for the formation

---

[1] *Canons* are a group of priests, gathered in what is called a *chapter*, who live a semi-monastic life at the cathedral church. This community gathers for communal prayer, the Liturgy of the Hours, and cathedral ceremonies. They serve as counselor to the bishop and oversee the governance of the diocese when the see is vacant. For a period in centuries past they elected the bishop. Chapters of canons at the cathedral church are foreign to United States church experience and are more common in Europe. In place of canons, the United States bishops have diocesan consultors, respected priests appointed by the bishop to govern the diocese when the see is vacant, which is the only function of the consultors.

of clerics. These cathedral schools were a somewhat more formal structure for clergy formation but were also uneven in their effectiveness. In the last quarter of the twelfth century, Lateran Council III made it mandatory that a cathedral school master for cleric formation be appointed and supported by a regular income. Lateran IV in 1215 made it mandatory that this cathedral school master be a theologian and directed that clerics be taught particularly the Scriptures and pastoral theology. From the thirteenth century forward, especially at Paris, Bologna, Rome, and other university cities, clerics destined for diocesan ministry were also prepared in the great universities. Still, diocesan clerical formation remained different from diocese to diocese across the centuries.

The seminary system took the more institutionalized form we know today when Pope Pius IV established a seminary at Rome in 1565 as a model of what the Council of Trent proposed for all dioceses. An outstanding proponent of seminaries after Trent, St. Charles Borromeo (1538–1584), cardinal-archbishop of Milan, established three of them for his diocese: one for older men, one for adolescents, and one for younger boys. This three-school pattern, modified by the French during the seventeenth century, took root in the Church as the formal seminary system. It grew over the eighteenth and nineteenth centuries and was solidly in place through the 1960s. It divided total seminary formation into two phases of twelve years' duration in two or three consecutive institutional settings.

### ii. The Minor and Major Seminary

The minor seminary, the first six years of formation, began after elementary school, when an adolescent boy was thirteen or so, and ended with adolescence, when a young man reached about twenty. These six-year schools, approximating high school and the first two years of college, taught the seminarian the fundamentals of faith, Latin, the humanities, and comportment. The young men generally lived a community life and boarded at the school.[2] They gathered daily for morning

---

[2] Mary L. Gauthier, ed., *Catholic Ministry Formation Enrollments: Statistical Overview for 2001–2002* (Washington, D.C.: Center for Applied Research in the Apostolate, Georgetown University, March 2002) 2–13, is the resource for the statistics in this section. The Center for Applied Research in the Apostolate (CARA), among other things, reports statistics for seminary formation. See them at www.cara.georgetown.edu. In 1967 the United States had 36 diocesan and 86 religious high school seminaries, 17 junior college seminaries, and 38 combined high school and junior college seminaries. In 2001–2002 there were 8 high school seminaries with a total enrollment of 816 students. To look at these statistics from a different angle, in 1967–1968 there were 15,823 high school and 13,401 college seminarians in

prayer, evening prayer, meditation, and mass. They also had a weekly conference from the head of the seminary, the rector,[3] and one from the priest in charge of their spiritual formation, the spiritual director. A yearly retreat was also customary, and later mandated. Through the early 1960s in the United States, except for large-city day school seminaries, seminarians were allowed to go home only on holidays and for the summer. All seminarians, however, no matter whether in boarding or day school, were expected to remain in close connection with the priests of their home parish and one another during their free time.[4] Dating by seminarians was forbidden.

The major seminary, the last six years of formation, began in mid-college. The first two years were dedicated to the study of philosophy, particularly the Aristotelian classical realism of St. Thomas Aquinas. The last four years were focused on theological study in immediate preparation for ordained ministry, including Scripture, history, doctrine, moral theology, liturgy, and canon law.[5] The daily regime was essentially the same as that of the minor seminary but more strictly kept. Seminarians most often wore the Roman cassock for classes, formal occasions, and generally on seminary grounds.

### iii. The Seminary System Today

Though in continuity with it, the clergy formation program in the United States today is more relaxed, more open than the former system. It is split into four levels: high school, college, pre-theology, and theology.

---

the United States. In 2001–2002 there were 816 high school and 1,594 college seminarians in the U.S.

[3] In Roman Catholicism this term is used for a priest whose office is exercised in place of the bishop. Thus the head of the seminary and the pastor at the cathedral church are called *rector.*

[4] As late as 1966, Quigley Preparatory Seminary in Chicago scheduled classes Monday through Wednesday, Friday and Saturday. Thursday, the customary day off in Rome, the seminarian was encouraged to spend time in his home parish. Sunday the same was expected—which led many seminarians to rectory basements to count the parish's Sunday collection.

[5] In 1967–1968 there were 4,876 diocesan theology students in the United States. In 2001–2002 there were 2,621 students enrolled in 47 institutions. Theology students studying for religious orders have witnessed an even greater drop, from 3,283 in 1967–1968 to 963 in 2001–2002. For the 2002–2003 school year, CARA reported that there was a drop of 170 theologate students between that year and the year before. The number of collegiate seminarians hit a modern low of 218 down from the year before. See "Signs of the Times," *America* (vol. 188, no. 17, May 19, 2003) 5.

The high school seminaries number only eight. The college level seminaries follow one of three models. The *free-standing* college seminaries, seventeen in all, offer a fully accredited academic program for undergraduate education, with an emphasis on philosophical study and seminary formation.[6] The *collaborative* college seminaries, twenty-seven institutions, are typically houses of formation where the seminarians live in community for formation purposes but attend an accredited undergraduate program at a Catholic college or university.[7] The third kind of college level program, the *religious house of formation* model, is typically sponsored by a religious order and comprises a small number of students living in a religious community attending classes at a collaborative or free-standing college seminary.[8] Sixty-nine of this model of seminary formation program exist in the United States.

The pre-theology programs were initiated in the late 1970s to meet a special need. These programs are for men who have an undergraduate degree but who have had neither seminary formation nor the requisite humanities, philosophy, and religious studies background to study theology at the graduate level. Some pre-theology programs are housed at college programs, some at school of theology programs. These programs can typically last one, two or, in rare cases, three years.[9]

The graduate level seminary, the *school of theology* or *theologate,* offers the graduating student the accredited master of divinity, which is typically a three-year degree. Catholic seminary takes one year more than Protestant seminary because of the liturgical and canon law requirements for ordination in the Catholic Church. Other graduate level degrees are offered along with the master of divinity in many institutions but require extra work beyond master of divinity study. No matter how much education a candidate may bring as he enters seminary formation, ordinarily two years in a school of theology are required for ordination because of what the bishops regard as every candidate's need for solid spiritual formation, which the bishops would maintain only seminary formation can provide.

---

[6] The free-standing college seminary enrollment in 2001–2002 was 854 students.

[7] The collaborative college seminary enrollment in 2001–2002 was 550 students.

[8] The enrollment in these programs in 2001–2002 was 120 students.

[9] The enrollment of pre-theology students in 2001–2002 was 725 students, approximately one-fifth of all theology level seminarians.

### *iv.* Program of Priestly Formation

All seminary formation programs in the United States are governed by a document published by the United States Conference of Catholic Bishops, *Program of Priestly Formation (PPF).*[10] This document, now in its fourth revision, is normative for seminaries across the country. It is dependent on documents from Vatican Council II, particularly the Decree on the Training of Priests and on the *Ratio Fundamentalis Institutionis Sacerdotalis,* which the Vatican issued in 1970, then revised and issued in 1985. These provide guidelines to help national conferences of bishops establish their formation programs. The current volume is especially indebted to *Pastores dabo vobis,* an apostolic exhortation on seminary formation issued by Pope John Paul II in 1992. The Pope's exhortation is cited 90 times in the 220 footnotes of the current *PPF.*

The *PPF* describes the total seminary formation program in general. In its current revision, it offers a glimpse into the contemporary concerns of the U.S. bishops through two special emphases. The first point of emphasis is the identity of the priest. The first chapter articulates a doctrinal understanding of priesthood and offers a statement on the diocesan priest's spiritual life.[11] It contains all the major thematics we have already reviewed across the whole history of ordained ministry.

Two sub-points in the identity reflection are particularly telling. First, the text describing the relationship between priest and bishop uses possessive pronouns: in reference to priests, the bishop is "their bishop"; for the bishop, the priests are "his priests." Repeated throughout the document, the possessive indicates the symbiosis assumed to exist between priest and bishop in the clerical culture. Second, the text describing the indelible character effected by priestly ordination is especially strong: "Ordained priests remain sacramentally related to Christ and to his Church for life with a character that perdures into eternity."[12] While Vatican II soft-pedaled this form of the theology of the indelible character conferred at ordination, the *PPF,* declaring that the indelible character has eternal effects, is a particularly intense and theologically controversial form of the ancient indelible character theology. Both of these points offer a picture of the bishops' mindset regarding ordained ministry and

---

[10] *Program of Priestly Formation* (Washington, D.C.: United States Conference of Catholic Bishops, 1993) 122 pp.

[11] Ibid., 7–11.

[12] Ibid., 10.

suggest the concentrated and forceful attention the bishops are inclined to give to the formation of clerics.

The *PPF*'s second point of emphasis is a twofold concern about educational and formational preparation. First, addressing pre-theology programs, the *PPF* makes it clear that these programs need to provide not only solid academic preparation for theological study but also a carefully focused introduction to the spiritual life. The document suggests that neither of these can be presumed suitable from any other educational or formational program than the seminary. Second, the *PPF* also underscores the need for formation toward lifelong commitment to celibacy. To this end the document reflects on celibacy's meaning, treats practical perspectives on celibate living and then looks as well at admissions requirements and ongoing candidate evaluation in light of the permanent commitment to celibacy.[13]

### *v. Seminary Admissions and Candidate Evaluation*

The *PPF* specifies the requirements for seminarian admission and continuing evaluation,[14] both of which rest squarely with the bishop, who typically delegates the responsibility to a diocesan functionary called the *vocation director,* who manages candidate recruitment and acts as the bishop's liaison to the seminary, optimally in a cooperative and collaborative relationship with it. The vocation director carries the heavier burden in the admissions process, the seminary in candidate evaluation.

In articulating admission requirements for candidates, the *PPF* states that "caution should be the watchword and the benefit of the doubt given to the church"[15] in selecting and recommending candidates for ordination. Candidates should be personally balanced, of good moral character, and have the proper motivation. Their qualities of person should suit them well for priestly ministry. The application process calls for personal interviews with the vocations office staff, recommendations from pastors and teachers, academic records and test scores, together with a physical examination and psychological assessment. The document urges the vocations office and seminary to set clear standards for psychological evaluation of candidates so that their life experiences, interpersonal relations, sexual development, and family background are thoroughly understood and evaluated. If issues of concern surface, depending on

---

[13] Ibid., 16–17.
[14] Ibid., 95–104.
[15] Ibid., 96.

their seriousness, the candidate may either be rejected or asked to make a commitment to face and process the issues during seminary studies. The *PPF* is filled with cautions about seminarians seeking admission either after recent conversion to Catholicism or after having left—under whatever circumstances—a previous seminary program.

Beyond admission, the seminary evaluation system does the heavy lifting in sorting out candidate suitability. Evaluation of a seminary candidate, particularly on the theologate level, is intensive and done yearly. The process includes self-evaluation, peer evaluation, summer activities supervisor evaluation, and pastoral placement supervisor evaluation. Though the rector is responsible for the process, the whole seminary faculty joins in. Regarding evaluation and the seminary rector and faculty, the *PPF* states: "Those responsible should regard the matter of evaluation as their most important task."[16] Considering the heavy burden of administering a major formational and educational institution, or teaching theology, this statement expresses the bishops' understanding of the critical importance of evaluations. Rectors and faculties take it very seriously.

The evaluation process occurs in what is called the *external forum*. That is to say, it is based on externally observable speech and behavior, a standard kept most carefully. The rector has an exclusively external forum relationship with students, to the extent that it would be inappropriate for him to ask intrusive questions of them. This distinction between external forum, observable behavior, and *internal forum*, confidential matter, is intended to protect the sacredness of the candidate's spiritual direction relationship, even as it opens the candidate up to being evaluated on any and all speech and behavior outside that relationship. In a close community setting, with faculty living and eating and recreating alongside students, evaluation can create considerable pressure on a seminarian.

The evaluation process culminates in a yearly statement to his bishop about the candidate's suitability for ordained ministry, which is based on externally observable behavior. The evaluation letter "should state whether or not the candidates possess sufficient intelligence, personal maturity, interpersonal skills, common sense, moral character, and aptitude for ministry to continue in the seminary program" and, finally, to be ordained.[17] Negative qualities can lead to student dismissal in the short- or long-term. The *PPF* urges "a fair hearing" of the candidate in

---

[16] Ibid., 100.
[17] Ibid., 101.

ambiguous circumstances,[18] but the benefit of the doubt rests with the seminary, the burden of proof with the seminarian.

Anecdotally, the evaluation process typically works, and works well, unless certain obstacles derail it. *Priest shortage* has been one obstacle. Reasonably positive personal experience of a candidate and great diocesan need means that bishops sometimes will not accept a seminary's negative evaluation or will give the candidate the benefit of the doubt over the seminary. Occasionally the *seminary rector,* again because of his personal experience of a student, as well as bishop pressure, will give the seminarian the benefit of the doubt over a negative evaluation of a student offered by faculty members. Another obstacle can be *student cloaking* of elements of his personal history, ideological bend, or personality traits that only become obvious after ordination. Given that the seminary environment, especially among theology-level students, is one of constant evaluation, student wariness about revealing their true priorities and feelings is not uncommon, and it can result in erroneous perceptions.

Yet another obstacle that can derail evaluation is *ineffective psychological evaluation.* Sometimes seminaries fail to adequately establish standards for admission with their psychologist evaluator team. Psychologists also have been known to take a stand contrary to some seminary standards without its knowledge. In both of these circumstances, the seminary is unable to get an adequate picture of a candidate's personality and traits, and so a candidate can be approved for admission or for program advancement when he ought not be.

*Ideological commitment* on the part of a bishop or a seminary may also be an obstacle. A more traditional-leaning bishop, for instance, might feel perfectly at ease ordaining a limited candidate who prefers the Latin Mass and devotional spirituality when a seminary may recommend otherwise. Still another obstacle can be a seminary's or a diocese's *evaluation process quality.* Though this is infrequent, especially in our time, seminaries and dioceses have been known to establish an "adequate for ministry" standard that is, in fact, far from truly adequate. An example: accepting piety and kindliness as sufficient for ordination when pastoral leadership skills are deficient.

Whatever the pitfalls of current seminary candidate admissions policies and evaluation, the processes in place today are far superior to and more professional than the processes that were in place in the era prior to Vatican II. Then, in a tightly structured community setting, the need

---

[18] Ibid.

for a sophisticated evaluation process was much less. Requirements for ordination were little more than good physical health, reasonable academic competence and sound piety—not to mention, for some, connections. Today, in a somewhat more open formation system, admissions and evaluation processes are far more sophisticated and need to be so.

### vi. Sexual Repression

Those responsible for the seminary system, past or present, would deny that sexual repression was the aim of the seminary system. The truth of the matter is that sexuality was little understood in past times, and a thoroughgoing repression of sexuality was not the seminary's aim. However, contemporary psychology would certainly agree that sexual repression was generally the seminary's effect.

Before Vatican II, whenever one entered the seminary, it was an all-male environment. A seminarian's exposure to women, beyond his family, was typically the secretarial staff, food service staff, and the occasional teacher or professor. As late as 1965, for instance, in the day school secondary level seminary for the Archdiocese of Chicago, Quigley Preparatory Seminary North, no women were on the faculty.

From the moment of entry into the old minor or major seminary, the seminarian was forbidden to date. While it might be understandable that a given seminarian, for very serious reasons, in consultation with his spiritual director, might go out on a date in a given instance, dating was forbidden. Whether a boy was thirteen, physically immature, and utterly inexperienced sexually, or whether a man was twenty-three and a reformed rake, the rules were the same for all.

The minor and major seminary was, by definition, this narrow, all-male environment. The environment was established to limit contact, and thus temptation, for the young male. This way of structuring life was then considered to be a matter of simple prudence as well. It was also considered to be the appropriate environment in which to learn the virtue and attendant disciplines of chastity.

Since the late 1960s this repressive environment has relaxed. Women are integral to most seminary faculties and hold significant evaluation and formation responsibilities, including spiritual direction. The understanding of the different levels of seminary formation, coupled with a concern that healthy people be ordained, has also made a difference in what relationships with females look like for seminarians.

The high school seminary today is a time for the student to be inspired to leadership, exposed broadly to the life of the Church, and stimulated toward an altruistic disposition. This more attenuated sense of the high school seminary's purpose means that high school seminarians are allowed to date, though preferably monitored in consultation with a spiritual director. Even seminary boarding schools will set up events with local co-educational or girls' schools to allow a more realistic and age-appropriate experience for the seminary students. Relationships with female peers are recognized as necessary for healthy maturation as a human person in the high school years.

The college seminary, a formation program focused broadly on ministry in the Church along with priesthood in particular, tends to be more discouraging toward dating for the seminarian as the seminarian advances through the program. The collaborative seminary programs allow the seminarian abundant opportunity to study and socialize with women, and they welcome this experience. They tend to prefer that dating be monitored in consultation with a spiritual director, however, so the experience can become part of the formation process. Because most of the free-standing seminary colleges by their nature offer less opportunity for studying and socializing between males and females, these programs give the subject less attention and tend to take for granted student co-operation with policy. Both kinds of programs indicate clearly to the students that the farther along a student is in formation the less dating ought to be an issue.

The school of theology, which is immediate preparation for ordained ministry, prohibits dating. Indeed, a seminarian is expected to have a demonstrated history of chaste relationships—for a minimum of two years—before entry into the program. If theology students, even socially, were to frequent establishments associated with "the dating scene," for example, certain bars, they risk dismissal.

Given the sexual repression inherent in the old minor and major seminary system, it was possible for a student to never confront the confusing and unsettling realities of human sexuality, including even so basic a concern as the seminarian's own sexual orientation. Even for the student who entered the seminary program at an older age, the seminary used to be the perfect place, upon entry, to forever after avoid sexuality concerns. Some candidates have likely used the seminary for precisely this purpose.

The modest admissions and evaluation standards for candidates in the former era, under the umbrella of a system that tended to repress sexuality, prolong adolescence, offer a secure constellation of lifetime relationships, and guarantee livelihood for a lifetime, were a major contributor to the sexual abuse scandal in our time. Careful study of the data would make it clear that most of the priest predators we have read about were formed well before the current, more nuanced, more realistic policies and processes set in place during the late 1970s and early 1980s. The changes in the seminary since the late 1960s, especially the more recent ones, are a very significant contributing factor to why some 98 percent of Catholic clergy today seem to be emotionally healthy men who are quietly about the business of preaching, teaching, presiding at the Eucharist, and leading faith communities across the United States.

### vii. Conclusion

Seminary formation of the clergy has always fallen under the diocesan bishop's aegis in a very personal way. Though it has not always been so, the formation of priests is a responsibility the bishops today take very seriously. Some on the left would regard seminary formation as broken because it occurs in an environment utterly unlike what the ordained will face in ministry. Bishops and rectors are often relatively defensive about the seminary's effectiveness. But whatever an individual bishop's or priest's point of view, the current way of clerical formation is the object in our time of continuing reflection by the national conference of bishops. A visitation of all seminaries in the country, for instance, is scheduled for 2004 by Vatican request made after the meeting with the American Cardinals and the USCCB officers in April 2002. The bishops will carefully structure this Vatican mandated visitation, guard closely their hegemony over the seminaries, and will do so with strong Vatican support, even in the event of a gentlemanly "veiled from the public eye" Vatican critique.

## B. THE ONGOING FORMATION OF PRIESTS

Dioceses across the country today generally understand that priestly formation is ongoing, never-ending, continuing after ordination. However, the shape of this continuing formation varies considerably from diocese to diocese, and it is most often quite loosely supervised. Even in the largest dioceses in the country, the person responsible for the continuing education of priests typically holds the position only part-time, often combined with the work of priest personnel, or vicar for clergy, or bishop's secretary.

The United States Conference of Catholic Bishops document governing the continuing education of the clergy is *The Basic Plan for the Ongoing*

*Formation of Priests.*[19] The document defines ongoing formation as "the continuing integration of priestly identity and functions or service for the sake of mission and communion with Christ and the Church."[20] This document is a probing, perceptive, warm, user-friendly, exhortative document that calls the priest to accept ongoing responsibility for his own personal, ecclesial, and social formation as an adult, as a Christian, and as a member of a particular presbytery. The document understands this responsibility to be accepted through both a priest's commitments and his participation in some programs. The document demonstrates a rich understanding of, and deep compassion and personal care for, priests. An altogether less nervous document than the *PPF*, it quotes Pope John Paul II's *Pastores dabo vobis* only twelve times in its mere thirty-four footnotes.

Appendix 3 summarizes the basic plan the document offers for the ongoing formation of the individual priest. The plan offers a comprehensive view of the priest's practical tasks and challenges, temptations and graces, as well as the discernment he needs to do in his life. It also emphasizes the five life events that may require a priest's programmatic attention: departure from the seminary, change of assignment, the first pastorate, mid-life and senior clergy status.

The plan also includes a reflection on formation for a divided diocesan presbytery.[21] It articulates seven factors contributing to such division: competition/comparison among males, generational differences, ambition to advance, lack of support from the bishop, widely varying backgrounds among the priests, differing theologies and spiritualities, differing languages, cultures, and places of origin. As a remedy for this lack of unity, the document suggests that priests pray alone and together, study and plan together, have informal contact and work to link across the various categories in which they find themselves. It also encourages the "unofficial" leaders of the presbytery—men with a proven track record, widely respected by their peers, and people who tend to gather others around themselves—to lead toward unity.

For as gracious as *The Basic Plan for the Ongoing Formation of Priests* is as a document, and for as penetrating an analysis of presbyteral life and formational need as it offers, ongoing formation is, in fact, sketchy across the 195 dioceses of the United States. Retreats are universally of-

---

[19] *The Basic Plan for the Ongoing Formation of Priests* (Washington, D.C.: United States Catholic Conference, 2001) 112 pp.

[20] Ibid., 11.

[21] Ibid., 93–103.

fered and priests are expected to participate in one yearly. Spiritual directors are available for priests, especially in the larger dioceses, at the priest's own expense. All dioceses offer an event, or two, or three each year for all the priests on some theological, spiritual, or planning topic. These events might be of a single day's duration, or several. Some are required, some optional. Dioceses, educational institutions, program centers, diocesan newspapers, and national Catholic magazines publish continuing education courses and workshops available to priests locally and nationally. Many dioceses offer the priests sabbaticals; these several-month to year-long opportunities for continuing formation can be formally academic, informal, or a combination of the two.

In the main, however, it is fair to say that diocesan ongoing formation for priests is relatively modest, not absolutely required, and calls for minimal accountability. With few exceptions, taking advantage of opportunities for ongoing formation is largely left to the initiative of the individual priest.

## C. CONTRADICTION ONE: FORMED INSIDE CLERICAL CULTURE FOR RESPONSIBILITY OUTSIDE IT

Seminary education takes place in a faith community setting designed to form priests not only intellectually but also spiritually and humanly. The seminary remains in our time a total-person experience that aims to teach the would-be ordained what they need to know, what they ought to value, and how they ought to think, speak, and act. In times past some seminaries even had a class on manners. Seminary also encourages the students to build the network of personal relationships within the clerical culture that will sustain them throughout their ministry. Priests lead the seminary faith community, largely staff it, and evaluate candidates' suitability for ministry. The seminary has been and remains a mostly male experience.

Seminary is a form of what anthropologists might call a male initiation rite. Elder males withdraw the initiate from ordinary life and take him into their care. They teach the initiate the stories, give him the experiences, have him perform the feats, and celebrate with him the rituals that are meant to forge him into a new, mature identity. The men carefully circumscribe the role of women in the initiation process. At the end of the process, the whole community gathers to celebrate the initiate's final rite of passage, his coming into a new way of being within and for the sake of the whole community. The Church calls this final rite of passage *ordination*.

Ordination establishes the priest as a new being with esoteric power and community authority. Clothing that sets him apart and identifies him with the universal priestly caste, to which he now belongs, publicly designates his new status. The clerical culture then sends the ordained to a particular community of often thousands of men, women, and children of all ages and walks of life. It authorizes him to lead but requires him to live apart, most often alone.

The people with and among whom the ordained serve are typically preoccupied by matters of day-to-day existence: birth, death, sickness, arguing and reconciling, falling in and out of love, hospitality and farewell, sustaining their own and their families' lives. They are also distracted and consumed by American popular culture and its values. The ordained are sent to call the people to conversion of life in Jesus Christ and to inspire, lead, and walk with them in their efforts to sort through the gifts and demands of their relationship with God. Many among the faithful are hungry for what priests have to offer and look to priests to show them the way to greater meaning, brighter hope, and deeper peace. Many of the faithful relegate their religious commitment, along with priests, to the margins of their existence. In the enormous tension of these circumstances priests spend their lives.

For all they have in common, priests are a highly varied group. Yet, in the main, they come to leadership with theological education, extensive relationships with bishops and fellow-priests, institutional loyalties, and both personal and institutional administrative aims largely foreign to the experience of those they serve. The concerns that rivet the lives of the faithful priests experience mostly on the margins of their own, and so priests understand these realities, for the most part, only vicariously. In priestly eyes, their own education and experience prepare them to do it all, or at least open up for them the resources for doing it all. But no matter how respected or appreciated a priest may be, those with and among whom he ministers tend to regard him as living on the margins of life, as a little out of touch.

Many of the laity tend to think priests somewhat elitist because of their knowledge, subtly aloof because their primary relationships are often elsewhere, and relatively inscrutable or tedious because of their institutional loyalties. Even if a priest is something of a rebel, he tends to define himself in relationship to the institution, thus keeping it dominant in his life. Many faithful think priests tend to dismiss their aspirations and opinions because the priests are so deeply committed to the institution's or their own aims.

More awkwardly still, the encapsulating preparation that is the seminary leaves a priest constantly tempted to focus his attention and energy on perception and image—his own, his caste's, and the Church's—whether that be in cooperation with or rebellion against, frankly. Priests often take care to preserve appearances while avoiding, escaping from, or cloaking the quandaries, doubts, and holes in their own minds, hearts, and souls. Yet, many lay people often experience priests as holding themselves up before the laity, even if only implicitly, as people who have it all wrapped up in tidy packages, rather than as brothers and fellow-searchers.

In summary, because of the nature of preparation for ordained ministry, the people with and among whom they serve see in priests both presumption and a certain naiveté. What the laity see in priests typically conflicts with priestly self-perception, but that's no matter to most priests. In true male form, if a priest says it doesn't exist . . . well . . . then it doesn't exist, does it? But there's the rub!

## D. CONTRADICTION TWO: PROMISED TO CELIBACY BUT ILL-EQUIPPED TO LIVE IT

When a priest promises celibate chastity, he pledges that his relationships will be free from sexual activity and that he will discipline himself to personal and consensual patterns of thought, word, and action that will preserve his chastity.

Those who will be ordained priests promise celibacy at the time of diaconate ordination—twice. Shortly before ordination, with his hand on the Bible, he reads and signs a formal, dense, nervously worded vow chart in a small, semi-private ceremony in the seminary chapel. He then promises celibacy much more simply in the ordination rite itself. From that moment forward, the priest is on his own. The truth of the matter is that he always was on his own.

When I was a seminary spiritual director in the 1980s and early 1990s, celibacy formation consisted of one month-long workshop in the second year of graduate school and occasional spiritual conferences throughout the four years. That was more than I received a decade and a half earlier. Though we repeatedly assured the seminarians of confidentiality, pervasive concern about the seminary evaluation process stunted deep, personal conversation. Some seminarians shared vague, generalized heterosexual struggles with chastity. Open admission of homosexual orientation, however, was assumed to put ordination in jeopardy, much less an ecclesiastical career, so the issue very rarely arose in conversation. Homosexual orientation remained essentially a matter confined to spiritual direction and the rumor mill.

Much good content was shared with the seminarians in the celibacy formation programs. Still, on the whole, celibacy formation was partial, superficial, nervously hesitant to ask the students to more freely and compassionately share with each other their beliefs, experience, and aspirations. It challenged the seminarians' minds some, while touching their hearts and souls very little.

How well-equipped are priests for celibacy in an ongoing way? Frankly, though they may receive occasional encouragement from classes, workshops, retreats, or books, but for some sharing with close friends and perhaps their spiritual director, priests remain on their own after ordination. Furthermore, most people today believe that priests have a higher proportion of homosexually oriented men among them than the rest of the population. Yet priests hold the same common prejudices against homosexually oriented men that society does, and they do next to nothing to lift the stresses that homosexual priests may bear because of rejection, isolation, or shame. The homosexual priest most particularly is on his own. Worse still, some priests carry singular burdens of complex attractions, confused feelings, and devastating sexual experiences in their past. They, too, are on their own.

Psychologists who are expert in the area of sexuality tell us that, in our culture, most people feel vulnerable when they talk about sex because most everyone is closeted about *something* in their sexual lives: orientation, particular experiences, unusual practices, unfaithfulness, lack of experience, performance concerns, etc. One in four women and one in seven men in the United States, for instance, have been sexually abused at some point in their lives. The experts tell us as well that people typically under-process and under-communicate about sex. Married people feel vulnerable around sexual matters as much as celibates, women as much as men, adults as much as children.

In our society we tend to hide our sexual beliefs, to be out of touch with our sexual feelings, and to be withholding about our sexual experiences. Most people in our society are sexually on their own. Still, given the central and public role that sexuality plays in a priest's life commitment, there's no feeling better about himself simply because he has lots of company!

# 7. Priest Accountability

## A. THE BISHOP AND THE CHANCERY

A diocesan bishop holds supreme executive, legislative, and judicial authority in his diocese. The universal law of the Church, Vatican interpretation of that law, and those common agreements designated as mandatory by the United States Conference of Catholic Bishops moderate this authority. Nonetheless, the bishop is in complete charge of the flock entrusted to him. The diocesan curia, commonly called the chancery[1] in the United States, consists of institutions and persons that assist the bishop in his governing role. The bishop appoints all members of his curia. They promise to fulfill their functions faithfully and to observe secrecy in accord with legal prescriptions and the bishop's own personal preferences.[2] The role of all chancery functionaries is to assure the common good of the diocese under the bishop's leadership.

---

[1] Historically, this word refers to the archives of documents. In ancient Rome a functionary, designated the *chancellarius,* was the doorkeeper who stood between the area of the court where the magistrate sat and the area where the people gathered. Standing at the gate, he collected the petitions and admitted the petitioners. During the reign of Charlemagne, the designation *chancellor* was given to civil functionaries who served the bishops as magistrates. In 1215, Lateran Council IV mandated the appointment of a chancellor, who also served as notary, in every diocese. The Third Provincial Council of Milan mandated the chancery as a place in 1573, and the place gradually became common throughout the Church.

[2] This promise raises interesting questions when considering the legal deal arranged with Bishop Thomas J. O'Brien of Phoenix. In June 2003 he relinquished his direct authority of oversight relative to sexual misconduct issues to escape indictment for obstruction of justice. This authority he delegated permanently (highly questionable in church law) to a "youth protection advocate" and the moderator of the curia, who is obliged and bound to act in accord with the bishop's mind. The youth-protection advocate is also a functionary of the Chancery according to the agreement. See "Agreement with County Attorney Regarding Sexual Abuse of Minors," *Origins* (vol. 33, no. 5, June 12, 2003) 68–71.

### i. Chancery Officials

The bishop's right-hand man is the vicar general. This priest, usually a canon lawyer, has executive power to act in the bishop's name, particularly in his absence, except for those areas the bishop reserves to himself or that legally require his mandate. The vicar general—and in larger dioceses there may be more than one—is legally bound never to act contrary to the bishop's will and mind. Episcopal vicars, who are assistant bishops,[3] have similar authority, but theirs is either more limited than the vicar general's authority or they are designated vicars general. Often the episcopal vicar's responsibility is restricted to a particular territory within the diocese, or type of business, or group of persons. There may be any number of episcopal vicars in a diocese, depending on diocesan need and Vatican appointment.

Most dioceses have a functionary entitled moderator of the curia. This priest, often the vicar general, or one among the group of vicars general in a large diocese, coordinates the administrative responsibilities of the diocesan curia and sees to it that the officials of the curia are fulfilling their duties. While the responsibility of this position belongs to the bishop, in most dioceses it is delegated to the moderator.

The left-hand functionary of the bishop is the chancellor. This position, most often held by a priest, but held by men or women religious or lay people in various dioceses, is legally responsible for the archive of the diocese, including all legal acts taken by the curia in the bishop's name. The chancellor is typically a civil or canon lawyer, or both. Assistants to this position, for instance people specializing in legal research or approval of marriage papers, are called vice-chancellors.

Every diocese also has a finance officer whose work is to administer the goods of the diocese in accord with the guidelines established by the legally mandated finance council. This functionary has only the delegated authority given by the bishop.

Present-day chancery staffs have evolved to include additional functionaries to meet current needs. One example is director of priest personnel, who consults with an elected personnel board. This full- or part-time role, most often filled by a priest, recommends assignment of

---

[3] These bishops are ordained to the full sacramental power of holy orders, and they are given a fictional diocese, that is, a diocese that historically existed but exists no longer, like Bardstown, Kentucky, or Natchez, Mississippi. As assistant bishops, their ability to function administratively depends entirely on the bishop of the diocese, called the *ordinary* bishop.

priests to the bishop, who has complete sway to do what he wishes with the recommendations, including ignore them. In dioceses with large numbers of deacons, one among them is typically appointed to assist with deacon assignments and oversee their formation.

Diocesan curia operations include two other major functions: the tribunal and the education department. The diocesan tribunal is a judicial body composed of a group of judges appointed by the bishop. It is headed by the judicial vicar *(officialis)*, a canon lawyer, usually a priest, who has delegated jurisdiction over judicial matters much like the jurisdiction the vicar general has over administrative matters. The tribunal's work may include criminal and other kinds of matters related to church governance. It is most often focused on marriage annulment cases.

The diocesan education department is a peculiarity of the church in the United States. Because of the massive commitment the American church has made to Catholic education and religious formation, the diocesan education office is often a major diocesan bureaucracy. This department typically oversees and offers resources to Catholic schools, religious formation programs in parishes, as well as youth and young adult ministry. Diocesan size and its commitment to education determine the scope and influence of the education office.

Other diocesan curial offices, like those of worship, marriage and family life, rural ministry or minorities, vary from diocese to diocese depending upon geography, demographics, resources, and priorities.

### ii. The Chancery's Functioning

The chancery's function and impact within the diocese vary from diocese to diocese and from one bishop to another. A strong, administratively oriented bishop may have a centralized diocesan structure, at the heart of which is a chancery running like a well-oiled machine: broad-ranging in its concerns, keeping the lid on some items and offering clear directives about others. A strong, pastorally oriented bishop may have a decentralized diocesan structure, one in which the chancery strives to serve priests and people but essentially stays out of the way. Other possibilities lie in-between. The Diocese of Pueblo in Colorado, for instance, where a pastor might be in a parish seven hours' drive from the chancery, will function much differently than the Archdiocese of Chicago, where all are within a brief commute to the chancery, depending upon rush-hour traffic. The largely rural Diocese of Des Moines, with 73 active diocesan priests, will function much differently from the urban

Archdiocese of New York, with over 563 active diocesan priests.[4] The bishop's personality, along with the size, geography, history, and administrative culture of the diocese, are all factors that shape how the relationship between the chancery and the larger diocese works.

For all of its services and functions, and all the attention it gets especially from priests, the chancery is not the focus of unity in the Roman Catholic diocese. It is the bishop. Whether he fits well into his chancery's culture or not, whether he prefers administrative to pastoral ministry, and no matter the chancery's size, the bishop is the unifying symbol of the church in the diocese. Moreover, the place where that unity is focused and celebrated is the cathedral, not the chancery; the central symbol of the bishop's authority is his throne *(cathedra)*, not his office. Second, whatever the bishop's style or preferences, however sprawling or modest the diocese or the chancery, no one at the chancery functions independently. The power of everyone at the chancery has distinct limits. Chancery staff members, including episcopal vicars, serve the common good of the diocese by serving the will and mind of the bishop since his alone is the fullness of executive, legislative, and judicial power in the diocese. All other power is vicarious, delegated. In every diocese across the world, the buck stops with the bishop. If it stops anywhere else, it is only because the bishop has delegated it to stop there. Rest assured that "anywhere else" is directly accountable to the bishop.

## B. CONTRADICTION THREE: ACCOUNTABLE WITHIN CLERICAL CULTURE FOR MINISTRY OUTSIDE IT

The bishop is in the highest box on the organizational chart for all diocesan priests.[5] While most priests take the opportunity when they get it to negotiate with the bishop, his disposition and assessment of a priest's abilities ultimately entrusts the priest with his ministry. This line

---

[4] These statistics, those of all the dioceses in the nation, as well as the personnel and institutions that staff every ecclesial institution in the nation, can be found in *The Official Catholic Directory: Anno Domini 2003* (New Providence, N.J.: P. J. Kennedy & Sons, 2003).

[5] "'I am going to make mistakes,' [Archbishop, later Cardinal George] Mundelein told His (sic) clergy on the day of his installation in Chicago [February 9, 1916]. 'But I am your archbishop, and I look to my priests to cover up my mistakes, not to expose, discuss, or criticize them. To whom else can I look for as much consideration? Your archbishop is the one man in this town who is constantly in the spotlight. Shield him as much as you can.'" See R. Scott Appleby, "Historical Overview: Priests in America, 1930–2002," *Origins* (vol. 33, no. 4, June 5, 2003) 53.

of accountability for pastors and other priests who are "in charge" of ministries is protected by canon, diocesan, and state law. For many dioceses, for instance, the parish corporate board is co-terminus with the parish corporation; they are one and the same. The bishop is chairman of all boards. The clergy have majority control. Regarding church matters—building, selling, spending large amounts of money, renting or leasing—priests in all ministries are answerable to the bishop. In some dioceses, notably the Archdiocese of Chicago, the whole diocese and all its ministries are a single corporation with a single corporate board chaired by the bishop. In any case, for the diocesan priest all lines of responsibility, even those mediated through others day-to-day, lead to the bishop. Whether loosely or tightly, all priests are held accountable.

The bishop and his staff minimally expect that a given priest will handle what he needs to handle in his ministry, if not to succeed, then at least to avoid church scandal and keep peace. However justified a priest may feel in a given instance, he knows deep down that if a parish or ministry matter gets to the chancery, he not only has to explain himself, but also somehow or other he has failed. Worse, the failure allows the chancery to tell a priest how it wants things handled.

For the people with and among whom a priest ministers, the world within and to which he is held accountable is as real as the Land of Oz.

At a noontime dinner following our parish's sixtieth anniversary, a companion and I walked from table to table, greeting people. When we arrived at one table, a senior woman immediately engaged me in conversation, then paused and said to my companion, "Oh! Who are you, Father?"

"I am Archbishop Flynn," he said with a smile.

"Oh! Nice to meet you, Father!" she responded. Clearly innocent of the clerical culture's consummate respect for an archbishop, she blithely turned back to me and continued her line of thought.

The basic assumptions of the laity are also thoroughly democratic. For instance, what most priests understand as holding confidences within the group for the sake of the common good, the rest around the table tend to see as secrecy, and often as an affront to spousal relationship. What priests understand to be participation together as the Body of Christ respecting appropriate roles—the pastor as head and parishioners functioning as hand, eye, ear, or foot—others tend to see as a lack of checks and balances. What a pastor sees as the prudent preservation of his ultimate responsibility for matters of law, finances, personnel, and faith and morals, others around the table tend to see as refusing to give people their rightful voice. Though a pastor or parochial vicar would maintain stoutly that the parish belongs to the larger diocesan church and the Church universal, the people think that the parish, like the nation, is theirs. Indeed, for some, the parish is the only sense of belonging to "Church" they have.

A deeply involved parishioner took it for granted in a conversation with our parish school principal recently that the principal's authority, and the pastor's, came from the people. The parishioner was, of course, gently informed that church reality is otherwise. Still, most parishioners really believe in their heart of hearts that the parish priest should be accountable to them. Explain as carefully and kindly as a priest might, the faithful in a parish community are inclined to resent it that their decisions are *merely* advisory recommendations. Bottom line, the people in the pews believe that their participation and financial support earn them a real say.

As a result, the faithful shut down when a priest, especially a pastor, blocks them from effective participation in real decision-making, manipulates decisions to achieve his predetermined ends, remains silent about what's really happening and why, offers them calculated ambiguity, denies reality, or simply fails to respond to their desires.

The faithful tend to see a priest's instinct for institutional preservation as narrow-minded and a thinly veiled form of self-preservation. It is typically suspect. The people feel insulted to think that the clerical culture would send them a pastor who has a history of hurting people or whose shelf life the bishop and most priests in the diocese take for granted will be only four or five years. The laity are appalled to think that if a seminary staff member, for instance, is found to be depressed or of diminished capability, then he is removed and sent to pastor a parish. The people in the pews would be shocked to think that mere availability and clerical politics are more important criteria for priest placement than a congruent fit between priest and parish. Yet, all of the above is the truth of the matter.

### C. CONTRADICTION FOUR: PRIESTS ARE DEPENDENT AND INDEPENDENT

On November 14, 1978, Franjo Cardinal Seper, prefect of the Congregation for the Doctrine of the Faith, sent Boston's Humberto Cardinal Medeiros an inquiry about Fr. Paul Shanley and his public statements contradicting Church teaching about homosexuality.

Cardinal Medeiros responded on February 12, 1979.[6] The letter is eight pages long. Cardinal Medeiros spends five pages recounting his views on homosexuality and his approach to the matter in the archdiocese. He addresses Cardinal Seper's original question in less than two pages. The letter includes seven substantial enclosures and a promise to come to Rome.

Cardinal Medeiros' letter is highly detailed, defensive in a genteel way, and somewhat obsequious. It is a model of what the twelve-step movement would call dependency. Yet no one in the clerical culture would question the independence of the cardinal archbishop of Boston.

Cardinal Medeiros was a product of the clerical culture. So are all priests.

Priests customarily defer to their bishop, or at least respect his office. Priests also customarily work around the bishop to get what they want. Most priests are closely informed about diocesan policy. They also expect exemption when they want it. Priests, especially pastors, are stewards of church worship and teaching. They also feel free to fashion worship to suit personal preferences and avoid moral subject matter that leaves them ill at ease.

I would offer an example having to do with Form III Penance (confession). This form of the sacrament of penance, commonly called general absolution because it is administered without the verbal confession of particular sins, is a sticky issue in the American church. Priests have made the judgment in many parishes across the country that, in accord with the 1973 *Ordo penitentiae,*[7] the conditions for general absolution exist because of the priest shortage and, in the judgment of some few priests, the relative lack of serious sin among the faithful who attend communal penance services. Hundreds of people in many dioceses come to penance services that offer general absolution. The experience can be most moving for both priest and penitent.

The bishops individually, however, and now the Pope in his motu proprio *Misericordia Dei,* issued in 2002, have been clear that the sacrament of penance may not be administered in this way except in the case of imminent danger of death (meaning a battle in war, a dying breath, etc.) or grave necessity (meaning an objectively exceptional situation in which the penitent would be deprived of the sacrament "for a long

---

[6] *The Boston Globe* investigative staff, *Betrayal: The Crisis in the Catholic Church* (Boston: Little, Brown, 2002) 235–42.

[7] "Rite of Penance," *The Rites* (Collegeville: The Liturgical Press, 1990) 376–79.

time," a judgment that can only be made by the diocesan bishop). Priest shortage is insufficient reason for Form III Penance; certainly the judgment about the seriousness of peoples' sin is tenuous at best. The bishops and the Pope insist, consequently, that one-to-one confession of sin is a necessity for the administration of this sacrament.

In the midst of this tension, but at some distance from it, a particular parish, like some eighty others in the diocese, had been doing Form III Penance for fifteen years. While the pastor was on sabbatical, the bishop did a little fishing in a conversation with his substitute, who felt uncomfortable about following the practice, and learned about the planned Form III. The bishop intervened. He chided the parish liturgist on the phone, called confessors himself, and then went to the parish to preside, preach, and hear confessions at the service. The pastor, fifteen hundred miles away but fully informed, was, of course, quite irritated by the situation. He prepared himself to give the bishop an ear- or eye-full, but the bishop never "sent a letter"—a loaded little phrase. In the clerical culture it is among the unwritten rules that a priest only writes what he is prepared to live with thirty years from now because most everything is placed in his file for future reference; if he is written to, he is obliged to cooperate, or see the bishop and then cooperate.

Five years later, Form III Penance remained parish practice. Why? The pastor says, "The bishop got his fingers into everything—and publicly—but he never came out and said 'no' to the legal parish administrator, he never wrote a letter, he never engaged me personally. So, I feel perfectly free to exercise my pastoral judgment."

## D. CONTRADICTION FIVE: SHEPHERD OF THE FLOCK AND CORPORATE CEO

The Church teaches that the priest, as co-worker with the bishop, serves Christ as teacher, priest and king. Priests have a share in the ministry of Christ and are ordained to build the Church into the Body of Christ and temple of the Holy Spirit.[8] The ministry of priests is to proclaim the Gospel of Jesus Christ, shepherd the people of a given faith community in communion with the bishop and the presbytery of the local church, and preside in sacrament, particularly the Eucharist. In-

---

[8] Austin Flannery, o.p., ed., "Decree on the Ministry and Life of Priests," *Vatican Council II: The Conciliar and Post Conciliar Documents,* rev. ed. (Northport, N.Y.: Costello Publishing Company, 1992) 863.

deed, the Eucharist is the fountain and the goal of a priest's ministry: all a priest says and does is ordered to the Eucharist.[9]

The people commonly consider the priest *in* the world but not *of* it, a fellow sheep, yet set apart as teacher, shepherd, and presider. The people most often respect the priest's word and give it weight. The priest is trusted, and his virtue is most typically presumed, even in the wake of the sexual misconduct scandal. The people commonly share with their priests in the sacrament of penance, in counseling sessions, and in social settings the most intimate details of their lives, from their feelings about their spouse and marital sexual practices to their innermost attitudes about their value and worth before God. They expect their priests to be physicians of souls, and so freely offer their hearts, minds, and spirits for examination and unction in the hope of healing.

It is a most amazing and wonderful experience to stand before an assembly and preside after years of being their priest. For a priest knows far more than he would care to know about many people in the assembly, often things that even spouses and children do not know. Consequently, to stand before an assembly and look into people's faces, and then call to mind people's joys and sorrows, delights and struggles, losses, grief, and hopes, is a deeply touching and sometimes overwhelming experience of intimacy, holiness, and grace. Being priest, being pastor, for an assembly of God's people is a constantly renewing invitation to compassion, understanding, attentiveness, discernment, awe, and tender love.

At the same time, the ministry of the pastor includes being CEO of a privately held corporation. Holy Spirit Parish in St. Paul, for instance, has 1,050 households with a school ministry program of 385 children. In the twelfth largest diocese in the United States, this parish is middle-to-small-sized. The parish reported in the 2002 fiscal year $17 million in physical assets. It would cost double that amount to replace the land and plant. The parish's cash flow is in excess of $2 million per year and growing. Because of recent facilities expansion, its debt burden in fiscal 2002 was approximately $5.9 million. Its endowments are worth about one-half million. The parish has 35 full-time and the same number of part-time employees. As pastor, I am responsible for it all.

As CEO, the pastor is responsible for all legal, financial, and personnel matters that arise in the parish. He is accountable to the bishop as chairman of the board, and to the other three board members—two trustees are parishioners, one is the vicar general—who constitute the

---

[9] Ibid., 865.

corporation. By canon law, the pastor has a council of parishioners to consult with him about financial and property decisions, and by strong ecclesiastical encouragement he has another council of parishioners who consult with him about parish planning and ministry management decisions. The diocese provides guidelines concerning precisely what financial and property dispersals require approval of the corporate board and the parish's councils. It is to these structures for governance, to a greater or lesser extent, that the pastor must give major management attention and his accounting. They are church and corporate structures.

In this rather thoroughgoing mix of pastoral and corporate responsibility, the roles of shepherd and CEO can be very difficult to hold together. When I first became a pastor, I asked a highly revered and venerable pastor what advice he might give. His answer conveyed the mix wonderfully well: "Be kind, say your prayers . . . and sign the checks!" The mix pulls at priests.

For example, Father L. sat in on school board budget meetings over a period of four weeks and, despite his kindly and consistent urging, the board was on the verge of approving a smoke-and-mirrors budget that included enrollment over-estimates, bloated administrative staff, and an inadequate tuition hike. After extensive talks with the principal and business manager, Father L. called an executive session meeting of the school board and informed the board that significant cuts would need to be made and a new tuition figure set. He then told them precisely what these needed to be. The board, taken aback, registered its discomfort. Father L. told the board members that if they had a counter proposal he was open to that. Because of the touchy sensitivity of the parent community, however, he insisted that the process be held confidential until a final budget was approved. One member of the board refused to keep confidence. Consequently, Father L. explained to the board that his cuts would stand. After the meeting, he spoke privately with the person who refused to keep matters confidential and told him that the next time he did that he would be removed from the board. Father L.'s budget was implemented. Imagine the body language, facial expressions, and inner ruminations of the board members at Mass the following Sunday as they replied, "And also with you."

After an extended, parish-wide consulting process, Father T. and the parish's councils reached consensus to build a new parish center. Mid-project, a council member came to him and informed him that the project was 8 percent over budget. Father T., assuming there must be some mistake, checked with the business administrator. It took the administrator two weeks and a meeting with the contractors to get on top of the figures. In the midst of endless construction details, the administrator had lost track of the money. The council member, meanwhile, began talking about the overage in the parish at large, and then publicly challenged Father T.'s integrity in a parish meeting. A fissure developed among parishioners, and even the chancery was drawn into the fray. By the time the dust settled fifteen months later, the council member had resigned and been replaced, four families had left the parish, and the chancery had answered the letters calling for his resignation by supporting Father T. The Sunday collection, which had gone flat, was coming back. Deep budget cutbacks had been implemented across the ministries. The business administrator had been encouraged to move to another parish. The pastor took full responsibility for everything, making a public apology for the overage in both a written report and from the pulpit. Parishioners report that Father T. was tense and melancholy as a presider for many months. He reports feeling deeply self-conscious and awkward at Mass, especially the Sunday morning Mass that the most upset individuals typically attended, because he could both see and feel many people's anger. The parish is unaware that the only reason Father T. did not resign is that, though it would have made life easier for him, it only would have made matters worse for the parish. The parish was also unaware of two more things. Nothing was harder for Father T. than presiding over an assembly that was mad. Second, the number of confessions dropped by about one-fourth.

Being shepherd of the flock and being corporate CEO creates conflicts that cost. Sometimes a parish will foot the bill rather than risk public argument, or it will not confront a major injustice because litigation is out of the question. At other times, as the examples illustrate, community unity and the sacramental life of a parish suffer because of corporate acts, or misuse of power, or because of misunderstandings that the CEO is unable to clear up because of his legal and moral obligations. Responsibility for law, finances and personnel, as well as for proclaiming the Gospel, shepherding the flock, and presiding at the Eucharist, is a juggling act requiring consummate skill, broad advice, and intense prayer. Even then, risks abound.

### E. CONTRADICTION SIX: PRIESTS ARE HIGHLY CIRCUMSCRIBED IN MINISTRY YET BROADLY TRUSTED

A priest's assignment to ministry has limits. The structure for getting an assignment usually leaves room for some choice on a priest's part, but for most that structure is but one element of the process. Availability, both the placement's and the priest's, is a major factor. But a given priest's reputation and others' assessments of a priest's abilities and quirks—that is to say, a priest's relationships within the clerical culture—also place limits on his assignment to ministry. Some priests, for a variety of reasons, get what they want simply for the asking. Others feel misread and ill-treated. Nonetheless, priests are, in the main, understood for who they are. Their ministerial style, if it is not respected, is at least typically accepted. Their superiors try to give a priest what he will at least agree to take. Besides, every priest knows that if the assignment doesn't work he can move. All of this treatment, though attenuated in some areas, is nonetheless a form of trust.

Priests are also limited in their exercise of leadership in parish and ministry life. The conduct of the liturgy, the configuration of the liturgical space, the ordering of ministries—all of these responsibilities have documentary explanations offered, limits imposed, results expected. Yet a priest is typically entrusted fully to implement church life across his ministry and is relied upon to remain sensitive to the Church, the diocese, and the local community in how he does it.

Priests are circumscribed especially in their administrative role. Canon, diocesan, and state law all hem in that role with expectations. Personnel, legal and financial matters, plus questions of faith and morals, are particularly sensitive, as are, of course, paying the diocesan assessment (a yearly tax supporting the diocesan ministries), the general insurance, the pension fund, and the bishop's yearly diocesan appeal. Still, priests are trusted to make sure that what is necessary gets done. They are also trusted to know when permissions need to be sought and expected to handle what difficulties arise. Most often a priest's superiors presume the best of him, accept his explanations, and offer him support.

Priests are also highly circumscribed by the expectations of the laity. When I was newly ordained and parishioners approached me with, "Oh, Father" this and "Oh, Father" that, I felt overwhelmed by the magnitude of their expectations.

The faithful expect Mass, sacramental ministry, accurate teaching, prompt and hospitable attentiveness to their needs, and a reasonable following of universal norms regarding church liturgy. They are excited about good preaching and increasingly expect it. They expect priests to be reasonably personable and have a listening ear. They expect priests not to get mad, especially at them. The people typically have their own sense of the parish's history that they bring to their expectations, and they presume a priest knows it, or soon will. The people in the pews expect to have their fair say in major decisions that will change parish life. They also expect that the pastor will not ask for more money than is necessary nor ask for money too often.

Parish and ministry staff members have expectations, too. They expect priests to be sexist, clerical, and concerned about power. They are delighted when they find that a priest is none of these things. Staff also expects that the priest will see to it that staff members are paid just wages. They also expect that the priest will offer charitable feedback, work closely with them when they ask it, and otherwise leave them alone to do their ministry. They generally expect, too, that a priest will not take too strong a public stand on birth control, abortion, or women's ordination.

Within all the fences they build around priests, those with and among whom a priest ministers offer the priest a breathtaking access to their lives, friends, families, history, desires, and innermost thoughts and feelings. The greatest circumscription and expectation of all is that the priest will treat their astonishing gift of intimacy with reverence, respect, and a sacred confidentiality.

In the face of all that limits priests, they are given wide berth and are enormously trusted. When a priest stumbles, he is most often offered generous forgiveness. There are only three things a priest must never ever do: express anger with physical violence, squander parish money, or abuse children.

# 8. A Priest's Personal Support System

## A. THE INSTITUTIONAL RELATIONSHIPS CONTEXT

From the moment of ordination a priest has a constellation of relationships that automatically attends his commitments. While it has some strong personal elements, this constellation is essentially professional. It is also defining.

### i. The Bishop

From a theological point of view, the primary relationship for the priest is with the bishop. This relationship is understood to be one of communion, support, and encouragement for the priest who joins with the bishop as a co-worker in the church for the sake of the Gospel. On a more personal level the relationship between a priest and bishop depends mostly on the bishop.

Some bishops develop a close bond with their seminarians and priests, having a strong, caring, personal rapport with them. These bishops know the priests and their families and have a keen enough sense of the priest, the assignment, and the priest's colleagues to be able to speak knowingly about a priest's gifts and challenges. These bishops often, by way of policy, tell their secretary, "If a priest calls and wants to see me, get him on the calendar as soon as possible." Other bishops may know most of their priests' names and be able to slot them in handy categories—one bishop understood his priests to fit into one of two categories: either one of "the big boys" or one of "those poor bastards"—but they, in fact, may have little personal knowledge of them, no informal rapport, and slight contact. Like corporate executives, these bishops tend to handle even major priest concerns in mere minutes. The priests who minister with these bishops understand that they should see "the boss" only when it is a must so as not to risk losing his respect or alienating him because of taking his time for what he might think trivial. Most every other possibility exists among the bishops as well, including bishops who play favorites of various sorts, some offering attention to the young and handsome, others to their old classmates, yet others to the chancery staff, still others to those priests with whom they worked or taught in previous assignments. All bishops, of course, pay attention to the "squeaky wheel," however they may think of him personally.

Though every priest expects at least a modicum of paternal care from his bishop no matter what his disposition, the fact is that the bishop's disposition toward a priest largely governs his relationship with a priest, not the priest's disposition. Priests respect this fact of their life, and bishops are content within it.

### ii. Other Priests

Also from a theological point of view, the next defining context of relationship for the priest is the priests of the diocese into which he is ordained. A priest's relationship with other priests has a major impact on his life. It can make a difference in the assignments he gets, what he is able to accomplish for his parish or ministry, and what response he gets when he fails in an assignment.

Shortly after ordination I asked an older priest, "Do the priests know each other pretty well?"

"No, but they know one another's reputation!" he responded.

Reputation can make or break a priest at assignment time or at the difficult moments of his ministry. It depends largely on the perceptions not of the ministry staff or laity but of other priests.

At the time of ordination, some priests have a wide knowledge of, and generous respect from, priests in the presbytery. If a seminarian is born and raised in the diocese, has been years in the seminary system, has good rapport with his parish priests and the seminary faculty, and participates in the wide array of seminarian opportunities and events, he may know better than half of the priests of his diocese at the time of ordination and have a solid reputation as well. If a seminarian is especially bright or competent, information that is usually spread by seminary faculty, placement supervisors, home pastors and bishops, then he may also come to ordination with high regard from priests. On the other hand, if a seminarian is born outside the diocese, enters the seminary program as an older candidate, or has but modest gifts, he may know relatively few priests and have little to no reputation at ordination time.

A newly ordained priest's first pastor and his constellation of relationships can also make a difference for better or worse in his life. Sometimes a colleague in an assignment later advances to significant responsibility, which can make a difference for a priest. So might an assignment that calls for the application of special skills that allows a priest to shine before his peers, for example, the young parochial vicar whose pastor dies and who manages the parish very well through the transition. Failing to get on well in an assignment with a priest who is highly regarded, or making serious mistakes in an assignment, can also shape the reputation and future of a priest.

Although many Catholics would likely not regard priesthood as a career, and many priests bristle at thinking of priesthood in career terms, ordained ministry nonetheless has about it many of the characteristics and pitfalls one would expect of any professional career. Though "advancement" for a priest in our time is hard to define—being appointed pastor of a large parish, seminary rector, member of the chancery staff, or bishop are all questionable advancement these days—still some priests are given most of the opportunities they wish, and others are given few because of their relationships with and reputation among their fellow priests.

### iii. Staff and the People

The colleagues and people with and among whom a priest serves in any assignment are also a major constellation of relationships for him. While shaping his life significantly on a daily basis, these relationships, for all of the joy and graciousness that can be found in them, require a priest's attention to professional boundaries.

Parish and ministry staff members are typically fellow professionals and theologians. The structure of relationship with them, however, is often given its primary contours by the priest's being in a supervisory position. These employment relationships require the priest to minister with his colleagues closely enough to establish rapport, grow in mutual respect, work collaboratively, and enjoy one another's company. At the same time, the priest supervisor must also plan and review ministry with a colleague, draw employment boundaries, reprimand and release from employment if necessary. In small staffs with close relationships, the line a priest walks in staff relationships can be fine indeed.

Especially since many priests have so much in common both by disposition and education with their fellow staff members, relationship with them requires close attention and considerable flexibility from staff member to staff member, depending on his or her area of responsibility and the disposition of the priest. One priest might work closely with staff members, regarding them as co-pastors in their area of responsibility, asking and using their advice. Another might prefer distance from staff and a relationship of bare professional accountability. No size fits all in shaping staff relationships because so much depends on a pastor's attitude toward staff, and vice versa.

Many volunteer ministers give generous, selfless service to a parish or ministry. Close relationships with them are also inevitable for a priest, especially, for instance, with parish trustees and council members. The quality of the volunteer ministry relationships, and their level of trust, can make a significant difference in the tone of a faith community and in what a pastor and the community are able to accomplish together. These relationships can often be closer than those with parish staff members for the pastor who shares a common vision with a group of faith community leaders and enthusiasm about the community's direction. Yet these relationships, too, need boundaries that support the role of pastor as leader of all the people who is available to all, not just some, people. Any form of exclusive behavior on a pastor's part, even with volunteer ministers in leadership positions, can build resentment and divide a faith community.

In sum, appropriate professional boundaries, respectful discretion, and congenial restraint in word and action demand continued monitoring on the part of all priests in their ministry setting. Keeping proper boundaries can be tricky; cool aloofness can be as damaging to a community as playing favorites. Nonetheless, healthy, balanced, attentive, and compassionate yet prudent relationship boundaries empower many priests, staffs, and people across the country to remarkable gospel ministry in their faith communities.

## B. THE PERSONAL RELATIONSHIPS CONTEXT

Though many priests and people would resent the statement and deny the fact, ordained ministry is surrounded with popular expectations and a sense of otherworldliness that makes truly supportive, intimate, and transparent personal relationships difficult for priests to find. Consequently, such relationships are limited essentially to three groups of persons. With the caveat that extraverts know no strangers and introverts use the word *friend* with the greatest care, and mindful that every rule has exceptions, the three groups are these: family, old friends and other priests.

### i. Family and Old Friends

An old friend made his first million before he was twenty-nine years of age. Many years ago now, while he was turning the bend toward his second million, he and I were driving to lunch one day when we fell into a conversation about a controversy he was having with his wife. He asked me what I thought. I thought he was in the wrong, but I hesitated.

"Greg, I am not sure I want to get into this," I finally responded.

"Mike . . . look . . . because of my money, as I grow older there will be fewer and fewer people in my life who will tell me the truth. You are one of them. I want to hear the truth. I need it. Tell me what you think."

Priests have a similar problem. They tend to receive deference and hold the power in a relationship because of their status. Consequently, family and friends who have known a priest from before ordination— and occasionally people who have known him for a very, very long time after it—are close enough to a priest's life, and beyond illusion enough, to give a priest frank feedback about his attitudes and behavior.

In 1998 I took a sabbatical during which I lived with my folks and read spiritual classics. Two months into the sabbatical, at breakfast one morning, my mother and I fell into a controversial discussion that got heated, then quickly cooled again. An unusual look crossed Mom's face.

"What is it, Mom? What are you thinking?"

"You know, Mike," she said, "I think that the parish is doing you a lot of good. You are actually becoming a nice person!"

Would that her remark were merely a tease!

In 1995 I was on the phone with an old friend complaining about my salary, lamenting that I had to pay 15.6 percent Social Security tax, put money in an IRA, try to tithe, and still have money for other things. Her voice seemed to tighten as we talked.

"You know, Michael," she finally said, "I don't think you have anything to complain about."

"What do you mean?" I said, eyebrows knit.

"What do you spend your money on?" I stumbled through a list that included toothpaste, shampoo, gas, clothes, shoes, and the car. "That's my point. You don't have much that you have to spend your money on, and your cash flow is at least the same as a person making $50,000 a year. As a single person, Michael, you are doing very well! I don't think you have anything to complain about."

Such punchy insight, frank yet kindly observation, and ease about driving a difficult personal point home can be the great gift of family relationships and old friends for a priest. Fellow staff members and parishioners typically have neither the closeness to nor the clarity about the person underneath the vestments to engage a priest in this way. For all of the swaggering to the contrary among staff members and parishioners, the road to truly supportive, intimate, transparent, and mutual personal relationships with priests typically includes a period of significant disillusionment with the priest and the church. Some relationships, when disillusionment begins to dawn, stop short. Some relationships survive it. Frankly, most relationships whither because of it.

### ii. Other Priests

Fellow priests are a natural group in which priests seek friendship, and many priests have priests as their closest friends. The seminary, which encourages and allows men to grow close with each other, and is the time during which many lifetime relationships are established, sets up the seminarian for seeking his primary relationship with other priests after ordination. The movement toward other priests for intimate friendship, consequently, is comfortable and compelling.

Beyond the seminary, friendships with priests for the newly ordained usually begin with the new priest's pastor and his constellation of relationships and then expand out to the pastors of classmates and their constellations of relationships. The yearly retreat, continuing education events, presbyteral convocations, ordinations, and the Mass of the Oils[1] are further contexts for meeting and getting to know other priests. Some priests get to know others through working with them on diocesan committees. The diocese affords abundant opportunities to work closely with priests who might join together to structure hospital ministry in the diocese, shape continuing education for priests, build the diocesan budget, place priests in assignments, or advise the bishop in his governing ministry. It is a fruitful avenue to get to know well a few priests at a time.

Other priests choose a more social route. They may play bridge together, golf, travel, have a book or supper club, or several of the above. In every diocese there are priests who are especially attentive to gathering

---

[1] The Mass of the Oils is a yearly event in which the bishop blesses the three oils used across the diocese in the sacraments. This celebration, specified in the Roman Missal for Holy Thursday but often moved to another day in Lent for the convenience of priests, usually includes some form of renewal of priestly ministry. It is typically a large gathering for diocesan priests.

priests together. Their hospitality can even be the glue that holds a diocesan presbytery, or large portions of it, together. All of these routes to friendship with other priests are readily available and well traveled.

A particularly important venue for priests to grow in friendship with each other is a priest support group. These groups, usually constituted by a small number of priests who pray, dine, socialize, and share stories together on a regular basis, are strongly encouraged in dioceses across the United States. Models for this kind of group abound, each emphasizing priest support from a slightly different angle. Support group offers priests the opportunity to share deeply with a few others their personal and professional joys and struggles, and then to hear other priests' wisdom and reflection in response. Many a priest has been rescued from personal disaster, many a ministry from community tumult, and many a staff member from inappropriate rebuke because of the attentive care and kindly wisdom of a support group. It is, for many, *the* important experience of friendship with other priests.

The bishop, the presbytery, the ministry staff, and parishioners form an outer ring circle of support for a priest's professional support. Family, old friends, and other priests tend to provide the sustaining inner circle of intimate relationships for priests. This whole galaxy of relationships constitutes the support system for most priests. In good times and difficult, how well a priest lives within this constellation of relationships has an enormous impact on his relative health and happiness and on all those who are engaged in ministry with him.

## C. CONTRADICTION SEVEN: WANTING RELATIONSHIPS IN MINISTRY BUT OBLIGED TO CAUTION

I offer this contradiction with a double caveat. It comes from the experience of a pastor who has been hurt and is consequently self-protective. It also comes from an introvert who is careful about using the word *friend* in any given relationship. What follows, then, may be less than universal, applying only tangentially to priests who are extraverts, in institutional ministries, have not yet led a faith community, or have not led in the heat of controversy. Though it may have limited application, I offer it nonetheless because it is my experience, and I hear it in others.

The people with and among whom a priest ministers—parishioners and staff—are often attracted to a priest for friendship, and priests are attractive. They are educated, fairly articulate, and have decent social skills. They are typically self-possessed and most often present themselves pretty well. They are usually competent at what they do. Many of them are funny, full of stories, and are generally "good guys." Because of the sensibilities that led them to ordained ministry, and because they work so closely with women—for instance, there are eight men on our parish staff of thirty-five full-time and thirty-five part-time ministers, four of them in maintenance—priests are often sensitive, attentive, and decently comfortable about listening to and expressing feelings. Priests often have more flexibility to keep company than most others as well.

Priests are also mysterious, fascinating. They are typically spiritual people, perceived as holy. The priest holds esoteric power and is regarded as having knowledge about the spiritual realm and wisdom about life. Most priests know the innermost secrets of many around them. They also hold a position of leadership that offers them real power to inspire people's minds and hearts. Priests are also celibate, a mystery in itself—and that means "available" to many in our American culture.

But close friendship with parishioners and staff, current and even past, can be a risky and awkward business, for a priest and for others.

Most priests are quite aware that more than a merely light and social friendship with them risks disappointment, even disillusionment. Allowing himself to be known well can compromise a priest's public authority as people find out that, really, he is just like them. A priest's saying and the people's believing the truth of that is one thing; having the details is another. Friendship for a priest can also take more energy than he has to give. Many priests fear hurting others because they get too busy or feel overwhelmed by their ministry. Friendship with the faithful, especially parishioners, can leave a priest at risk of taking advantage of the people's instinctively generous response to a priest because of his role. It can leave people at risk of feeling rejected when a priest has to say no. Friendships for a priest can create jealousy in the community he serves, tempt him to favoritism of various sorts, or create resentment and gossip.

Moreover, a priest's natural relationship tendencies are, of course, all too human. Sometimes priests, like everyone else, are tempted to use people to escape loneliness, grief, and occasional feelings of inadequacy. Sometimes a priest spills. Sometimes he has to withhold. Priests and people sometimes forget that priests are sexual beings. The immense trust of people can lead to the priest's gaining too close and too free an access. That access can risk a priest's compromising his sexual boundaries, stimulating his sexual fantasy, opening to sexual opportunity, tempting him toward sexual exploitation, leading him, if he falls, to ministerial and personal disintegration.

It has consistently surprised me that many of those I serve assume we are friends. Because a priest's self-presentation is so public, people think they know him. A priest knows inside that the people just might not. Many people also confuse the ministerial with the personal, thinking that a priest's tender concern is an act of personal friendship when its real significance, rather, tends more in the direction of pastoral care. This confusion can be quite painful in some relationships—for the priest and for others.

Close friendship is about open and intimate mutuality, commonality, and equality, people delighting in the same truth, enjoying one another's company, and sharing simple affection and fun. Friends are a great boon in human life and an enormous source of support that all human beings both need and deserve.

Yet the nature of a priest's leadership role in a faith community—and what's at stake because of it—means that the priest, especially a pastor, typically has to approach friendship with those beyond family, old friends, and fellow-priests with discerning reserve. In my experience people find this necessary reserve a sore point and hard to understand. Yet, when things get confused or conflicted, the responsibility for sorting through it inevitably falls on the priest.

## D. CONTRADICTION EIGHT: A COMMUNITY LEADER BUT PERSONALLY LONELY

Ordained ministry is all about relationships. Priests are called by God and sent forth by the bishop, in communion with the worldwide Church and the presbytery of the diocese, to a local faith community. There the priest is commissioned to preach the Gospel, teach the truth of the dying and rising of Jesus, preside at worship, care for the community pastorally, and be a model of the imitation of Jesus Christ in all that they say and do. They are sent to a people to be servant leaders who call the faith community to unity with one another, holiness before God, universal communion with the Catholic Church across the world, building up of the Kingdom of God, and continuity with the vast sweep of the Christian tradition. To these ends priests are educated and evaluated throughout seminary formation, offered continuing support and education after ordination, and are exhorted and inspired to persevere throughout their ministerial lives. Relationships, building up the Body of Christ, are what priestly ministry is all about.

The contexts of their ministry, the diocese, the presbytery, and the faith community, are a galaxy of relationships. Priests minister with individuals in their homes, in their ministry office, at bedsides and casket sides, in the reconciliation room, in the car, out at lunch. They minister with and among groups small and large around the dinner table, at meetings, in living rooms, at receptions, on the street, in the church. They carry a cell phone, or have the parish phone in their office and at home, to remain available to people. People call at 5:30 A.M. and during the night. The pink slips stand in stacks when a priest has been out, the e-mail messages line up. The daily mail can take an hour or more to read and offer response. Relationships are what a priest is for and shape the whole of a priest's life. In most of their relationship context, priests are expected to lead.

Yet many priests are lonely. Loneliness is part of human life at times for most people. A child on Saturday afternoon, the senior in an apartment or nursing home, the husband on business staying in a hotel, the mother who has recently sent her youngest off to school, the high school student who is being hazed—many people experience loneliness. But priests, whose lives are all about relationships, report that they feel lonely. Why?

United States priests suffer from all of the same cultural biases and strains as any American male. Wives structure the social life of the majority of married males in the U.S. It is typically the woman of the house who sends greeting and thank you cards, alerts her husband to the need to get together with particular friends, asks about and knows the news, and provides the energy for hospitality, if not doing all the work of it, then often teaching the males of the house how to do it. This kind of support and focus, except for the rare secretary or staff member, is closed for a priest. He is on his own.

Children often call American men into wider and more varied circles of relationship. Meeting and growing in friendship with others on the side of the ball field or court, working together on the school play, leading together in scouts are all venues for men to grow in relationship, especially with other men. These natural venues are closed for a priest, or only modestly available.

A priest's schedule is eccentric relative to that of the rest of the culture. Daily, a priest typically needs to be on hand for the 7:30 A.M. Mass as well as the pastoral council meeting that ends at 9:00 P.M. If he is free, it might be in the late morning or early afternoon, depending on appointments. Lunch anyone? During any given week a priest needs to be available when the people are. This means that his work is, ordinarily, evenings and weekends. That is when people are available for ministry, planning, and parish activities and functions. When people are working—afternoons, for instance—often a priest is free. When people are free, a priest is usually working. When people are celebrating holidays, priests are also usually working, and at their hardest, for example, Christmas and Easter. One of the most difficult dimensions of priesthood for my friends and me to get used to after ordination was the simple fact that when they were available I was working, and vice versa.

Most priests tend to overwork as well. Managing one's own time alone, having duties in the early morning and late evening, living on site, and needing to be ever-available all contribute to this tendency. Working too much means being on the job in excess of sixty hours per week. While some priests slack off, most work hard and are passionate about their commitments. Sixty hours a week, for months on end, can even be light for some priests. My worst work week ever was seventy-eight hours. Only toward the end of my ninth year as a pastor, with most of the heavy lifting done and funerals diminishing, was I able to keep the work week between forty-five and fifty hours. Many priests live under these same pressures.

The people with and among whom priests minister are generous in response to keeping company with priests. They invite priests over to relax, offer the cabin for escape, and extend wondrous hospitality. Few people understand, however, that leisure with a parishioner is work, not rest. In fact, it takes awhile for even the priest to understand this.

Because of these factors, when the world stops, what does a priest— a single American male who lives alone—do with himself when he has free time? Sometimes he sleeps to build a head of steam for the next round. Sometimes he zones out with TV. Sometimes he spends time with staff and parishioners talking business in social settings under the illusion that he is resting. Sometimes he does busy-work to fill time. Sometimes he engages in various forms of self-destructive and compulsive behavior for the sake of some minimal satisfaction. Often he doesn't know quite what to do with himself, fitfully sputtering like an engine in overdrive suddenly turned off.

One of the great challenges for a priest, then, is learning to live a balanced life of healthy eating, adequate sleep, regular exercise, generous time for prayer, ample time for friends, and grace-filled leisure time. Many priests fail to find rewarding and satisfying hobbies or leisure activities, have too few friends, or have friends on opposite schedules, and so they feel out in the cold when time is free, the day is done, or the weekly day off rolls around. In the midst of the pulls and tugs of ordained ministry, it takes deep commitment, strong motive, and steely determination to seize the time and structure the activities that can help bring balance to life. The constant need to remain flexible because of the accident, or funeral, or command performance in the parish adds to the strain. In the midst of the struggle, though they are leaders of community, many priests suffer from loneliness.

# 9. Living a Contradictory Life

## A. CONTRADICTION NINE: MINISTERS OF UNITY
## IN A FRACTURED CLERICAL CULTURE

In the high priestly prayer at the Last Supper narrative of the Gospel of John, Jesus pleads for his disciples and for us, the Church: "that they may be one."

> As you, Father, are in me and I am in you, may they also be in us, so that the world may believe that you have sent me. The glory that you have given me I have given them, so that they may be one, as we are one, I in them and you in me, that they may become completely one, so that the world may know that you have sent me and have loved them even as you have loved me.[1]

Unity among the disciples and in the Church is the deep concern the Gospel writer places on the lips of Jesus. Unity authenticates Jesus' mission and proclaims God's love for the Church. Indeed, unity is so critical that, though he draws a picture of a commanding and all-knowing Jesus, the writer of the Gospel of John is willing to put a tone of urgency and longing underneath the words of Jesus' prayer for unity.

For ordained ministers today, from the Vatican to the local parish, unity remains a primary concern.[2] A Christian or Catholic monolith is impossible and, for whatever the impressions to the contrary, has never existed. The word *catholic* itself implies pluralistic reality in the Church. Nonetheless, the ordained are ministers of unity and continuity in the Church, and a constant preoccupation of their mission is to keep unity in the community they serve: parish, diocese, and Church universal. Councils, encyclicals, magisterium teaching, canon law, liturgical rubrics and language, preaching, disciplinary guidelines, and even dress regulation

---

[1] John 17:21-23.

[2] *The Basic Plan for the Ongoing Formation of Priests* (Washington, D.C.: United States Catholic Conference, 2001) 98–100, cites both scriptural tests and John Paul II's *Pastores dabo vobis* to reflect on the nature and importance of unity in the Church.

all serve unity. Church and local community unity authenticate the mission of Jesus Christ and the truth of the Gospel, as well as bear witness to the reality that the community of faith accepts the gift of God's life and love. Unity keeps worship joyful, energy well-directed, the community growing, money flowing, and the Church moving outward to change the world. Disunity diminishes priest and mission effectiveness, undermines the comprehensive use of priest resources, stands as a contrary sign in the faith community, discourages potential priest candidates, shifts ministry focus from gospel mission to disputing over angels on pinheads and atomizes a parish, a diocese, or the Church universal. Building and sustaining unity is a large share of the work of ordained ministry, especially in positions of community leadership.

Though the ordained are ministers of unity, the presbyteries of dioceses across the country and across the world today are divided. This painful fact compromises priestly identity in the Church and impedes the effectiveness of the Church's mission. Nor will this disunity end soon if the history of councils and their aftermath has anything to teach us. However, the nature of this disunity warrants examination because it is so flagrant a contradiction.

The United States Catholic Conference of Bishops document *The Basic Plan for the Ongoing Formation of Priests*[3] offers a helpful diagnosis of seven contributing factors: competition, clerical envy, generational differences among priests, bishop support, varied priest background, differences of language, culture, and place of origin, as well as differing theological presuppositions and spiritual practice preferences.

### i. Competition

American males learn early in life to compare themselves to and compete with others. The baseball field and the classroom, our circle of friends, and the things they own can all be the basis for competition and comparison. This fundamental American cultural reality is natural for males, one element of why intimate relationships within any group of men can be so difficult in our society. Priests are no different in this regard.

Fathers Matt, Jeff, and Pat, for instance, are very close friends, and have been for many years. They enjoy one another's company, trust one another's judgment, ask one another's advice, spend regular time together, and share freely about what they think and feel, from the vicar general's role in the chancery to their personal sexual struggles. All three

---

[3] Op. cit., 95–100.

of them have built buildings during their pastorates. On this subject they remain awkwardly reticent.

Jeff built a parish ministry center and said next to nothing about it to Matt and Pat, who heard little about its progress and finally saw it only incidentally. Jeff asked Matt's advice about the dedication ritual, but he was clear that he might or might not use the suggestions. Then Matt built a parish ministry center with his parish; Pat did a year later. Both of them were steeped in the work but knew better than to talk about it much to the others. When the buildings were completed, Jeff never asked to see them and was relatively restrained in his response to the buildings when he did get a very "low key" cook's tour. Ironically, Matt, Jeff, and Pat were able to talk freely with each other, though, about the very indifferent reactions they received from other priests about the building process and the end product.

Though it tends to lessen with the passing years, most priests compare notes about Sunday homilies, collection figures, their command of their work, and the compliments they receive. Deeper issues are often treated more gingerly and with some restraint, however, because they can readily become divisive. Priests feel freest to compare with other priests when the person they are comparing with is out of earshot.

### ii. Clerical Envy

One priest in a Midwest diocese teases publicly that the dream of his life is to be made a monsignor. His bishop has confidence and congeniality enough to tease him back publicly, even calling him monsignor on occasion, and on other occasions threatening that he will never get purple buttons if he continues to behave the way he does. This playful exchange is generally received among the priests as a healthy and delightful one. It suggests, however, some awkwardness in our time regarding priest advancement and recognition.

In times past, becoming a monsignor was public recognition, usually from the bishop, of a priest's accomplishments.[4] A young monsignor was

---

[4] The Vatican, at the request of a bishop, grants designation as a domestic prelate, which is appointment as an honorary member of the papal household. The designation entitles the priest to be called "my lord," *monsignor* (the typical address for bishops in Europe), and to wear a black cassock with red piping, a fuscia sash and *feriola* (the cape worn, for example, by Bishop Fulton Sheen), and a black biretta (a squared hat with three upward flaps) with a fuscia pompom on it. To be "made a monsignor" is exclusively honorific. Sometimes a bishop or archbishop other than the diocesan bishop has a priest made a monsignor. This can be cause for some competitive stress between a priest and his own bishop.

understood to be on the road toward great responsibilities, like the chancery, a large and wealthy parish, or even the episcopacy. These days, what constitutes advancement or recognition among priests is unclear. A large parish can be simply more work. It makes no difference in salary. Wealthy parishioners can be more demanding than others. While some bishops recommend to the Vatican that priests be designated as monsignors, many demure. While some priests appreciate the recognition for themselves or another priest, others are jealous of it or disdain it. For many priests, even becoming a bishop is of no interest because it opens one to considerable pressure, headaches, and politicking in what is the most difficult and stressful ministry in the Church.

Lack of clarity about what assignations constitute advancement or recognition complicates the age-old fact of envy among priests. Consequently, possible causes for envy abound. Priests know who among themselves are the best preachers, the most effective pastors, the most grounded spiritual directors, those favored by the bishop, and those most likely to get what they want. They know who are wealthiest among the priests, who are the well-traveled and the best educated. They know the liberal, the conservative, the relentlessly middle-of-the-road, and who is darling to whom and who is not. They know who can make what parish situation work and who cannot, who will be able to retire early and who will not, who works and who does not. In the contemporary confusion about what advancement and recognition really are, all of the above, and many things more, can become sources of envy that divide priests.

### iii. Generational Differences

Within a given diocese, priests tend to represent four generations of formation. Vatican Council II is the reference point. Men ordained in 1963 and before were formed before the council. For members of the World War II and Korea generations, theological study was rather rote. They typically studied in Latin, out of formulaic theology manuals, and learned to preside in the Tridentine rite. Men ordained between 1964 and 1972 or so were in formation both before and after the council. These were exciting days of some theological ferment. Few of the men ordained as early as 1964 said the Latin Mass, though that is what they were prepared for in seminary.[5] Priests ordained after 1973 until the mid-1980s

---

[5] See Paul E. Dinter, *The Other Side of the Altar: One Man's Life in the Catholic Priesthood* (New York: Farrar, Straus, and Giroux, 2003) 41–70, for a sense of the seminary experience of this group of seminarians.

were formed largely in the post-Vatican II seminary. They are largely members of the baby boom generation. The critical question for understanding them is to ask: where were you in 1968 and 1969, and what did you look like? The priests ordained after the mid-1980s, especially those ordained in the mid-1990s and afterward, were formed significantly by the papacy of John Paul II. Many in this last group share more in common with some of the men ordained in the 1940s and 1950s than they do with the baby boomer priests.

While this breakdown is not a complete predictor of attitudes and behavior in priests, it is a handy rubric for understanding generational differences. For many priests, though certainly not all, to have lived through Vatican II is to have been inspired by powerful enthusiasm for change and lifted up by great excitement for the future of the Church. Even those who lived through Vatican II and dislike the changes invoke the council to explain their position. Many of the younger priests, however, especially those who entered the seminary during their early twenties rather than at an older age, bright and effective as they are, often tend to reach for and preach a clarity of theological, legal, and religious practice that, from the perspective of older clergy, neither life nor the Church offers.

The formation generations among the priests tend to get along in some dioceses and are distinctly alienated from one another in other dioceses. The bishop has the most impact on generational unity or disunity, and, whether they are hospitable or contentious, the same can be true of one or two strong priests who gather other priests around them.

### iv. Episcopal Support

It is an embarrassing fact that priests, as a group, tend to be a fairly adolescent bunch. They believe they should get what they want for the asking; they want to be taken care of and feel they have every right to make demands. The person toward whom all this adolescent energy is directed, of course, is "Dad," the bishop. Consequently, the bishop's attitude toward the priests of the diocese can bring unity about, hold a presbytery together only superficially, or allow a presbytery to divide or remain divided.

Some bishops attentively pastor their priests. These bishops are approachable, available by phone, patient listeners, good with names, remember personal details about their priests, and strive to be personally and professionally supportive. Priests are more like dukes than peasants. They can be imperious in their assigned domain and quite demanding. Yet some bishops foster unity among the priests simply by their compassion.

Some bishops take a strong stance about what they expect from priests and persistently nudge them to adhere to it. They do this by popular appeal and inspiring example, like the late Cardinal Joseph Bernardin of Chicago; or by staunch, outward-moving ministry in the public square (and some humiliation),[6] like the late Cardinal John O'Connor of New York; or by a more inward-looking mandating of certain theological and disciplinary requirements, like the late Bishop Glennon Flavin of Lincoln, Nebraska. This sort of bishop walks a line that can, with congeniality, compassion, and patience, unite a presbytery; the bishop can also, if he becomes self-righteous or rigid, divide the priests.

Some bishops tend to give the priests of the diocese a low priority and focus their interests elsewhere. Perhaps more oriented to chancery administration than personal relationships, these bishops prefer the company of lay people, feel confused about what to do to bring priests to unity, wantonly spend the good will of the priests, feel threatened by them, are angry with them, or feel drained by them. In the dioceses of these bishops, the presbytery, if united, is united against the bishop. Whether it is because of the bishop or the priests' response to him, these presbyteries live in a reality that drains time and energy from the mission of the Church, diocese, presbytery and bishop, and that reduces priests to arguing, for example, about Form III Penance, concelebrating (albs or no albs) when they gather, and petty matters of liturgical correctness.

Those bishops who work for presbyteral unity usually have it in their diocese. Those who work at unity half-heartedly, confusedly, or anxiously usually pastor a disunited body of priests. Lack of unity among the priests creates problems across the board for the bishop and the church in any diocese.

### v. Varied Priest Background

Varying background among the priests also challenges priest unity. In the past, most seminary students were approximately the same age— twenty-five or twenty-six at ordination. As late as the early 1980s, a thirty-two-year-old seminarian was considered by his peers to be rather old. Times have changed.

In 2001–2002, 13 percent of theology students were in their early twenties. Twenty-seven percent were between twenty-five and twenty-nine years of age, 24 percent between thirty and thirty-four years old, 18 percent between the ages of thirty-five and thirty-nine, 13 percent between

---

[6] Ibid., 155–57, 175–77.

forty and forty-nine, and five percent were over fifty.[7] These men have been lawyers, engineers, salesmen, teachers, and church ministers. They bring significant life experience and rich background to ordained ministry but sometimes little religious formation. One student seminarian I knew in the early 1990s had come to seminary formation at twenty-nine with no Catholic education, no religious formation since sixth grade and eleven years experience in the military. This kind of diversity offers remarkable assets to the church and to a presbytery. At the same time, such wide variance in background, experience, and values deeply challenges unity within a presbytery.

### vi. Differences of Language, Culture, and Place of Origin

Yet another kind of diversity that challenges a presbytery's unity is differences of language, culture, and place of origin. Until recently, the vast majority of seminarians were white—79 percent as recently as 1993.[8] In 2001–2002, while 66 percent of all seminary priesthood candidates were white, 15 percent were Hispanic/Latino, 11 percent Asian, 5 percent black, and 3 percent were other than these. At the same time, nearly one-fifth of all seminary students in the United States were from countries outside the United States. Some sixty-nine countries were represented among these students, and 53 percent of these students were studying for dioceses in the United States.

This particular diversity has proven controversial in some dioceses. Some bishops, responding to the shortage of priests in the United States, actively recruit foreign-born priests for ministry in U.S. parishes. While many of these priests make an enormous and colorful contribution to their local churches, language and culture concerns have created divisions between bishop and presbytery and among priests within a presbytery.

A priest friend in a western diocese received a call one day from a foreign-born pastor some miles away who had recently arrived in the United States and had just been appointed to the parish. As dean of the area, my friend supported priests of several counties in the diocese and advised the bishop, which is why he received the call.

"Father, who cooks for you?" the priest asked my friend.

"I do," he responded.

---

[7] Mary L. Gauthier, ed., *Catholic Ministry Formation Enrollments: Statistical Overview for 2001– 2002* (Washington D.C.: Center for Applied Research in the Apostolate, Georgetown University, March 2002) 7.

[8] The following statistics come from ibid., 8.

*"You* do? And who does your laundry?"

"I do," my friend responded.

Clearly the priest was amazed. "And who cuts your lawn?"

"Well, our maintenance staff does, though I do sometimes. It depends."

"Oh, Father, I am not used to all these things. I do not think I can do them."

"Then maybe you ought to hang it up and go home!" my friend affectionately but brashly responded.

The issue here is not only one of sensitivity, but also, some would argue, the theological implications of the definition of church and the role of the priest in the faith community. In response, many dioceses are taking constructive steps to provide newcomers personal support and help with acculturation. Nonetheless, language, culture, and place of origin are fault lines that can cause division among priests.

### vii. Differing Theology and Spirituality

A fundamental division among priests falls between the liberals and the conservatives, with the moderates in-between. But what do these terms mean? First, it is useful to differentiate between the American and ecclesial cultures for understanding the meanings of the terms. Second, an ecclesiological perspective helps in grasping the meaning of these terms in a Catholic context.

Since after World War II especially, when the American and papal flags were installed on parallel poles inside and outside churches, Catholics in the United States, like most Protestants, are generally more American than they are Catholic. That is to say, American cultural perspective has more hegemony over their working understanding of day-to-day reality than does Catholic cultural perspective. This American cultural dominance inclines most Catholics to hear the words *liberal* and *conservative* first from an American political point of view and then to impose that understanding on ecclesial realities. This rule of thumb confuses debate in the U.S. church.

Pope John Paul II has been highly critical of communism across the world and most effective against it. He has also been highly critical of capitalism, especially the free run of free markets. These points of view fit very untidily into American categories. Indeed, most Americans would assume they contradict one another. From the point of view of Catholic teaching, however, what the Pope articulates on both sides is bedrock social justice tradition.

Another case in point is life issues. The Catholic church across the United States and the world has taken a strong stance against abortion, capital punishment, and euthanasia. At the same time, relative to the euthanasia question, for instance, Catholic teaching is also clear that extraordinary medical means, of great cost, with little promise for reasonable quality of life, need not be applied; a person may be allowed to die naturally. These ecclesial positions, though coherent in the Catholic tradition, seem contradictory in American political culture categories.

Simply put, the terms *liberal* and *conservative* mean different things in American political culture than they do in ecclesial culture. To begin to grasp what the terms mean in ecclesial culture, one needs to abandon American political culture biases. Few do this easily or consistently.

When the terms *liberal* and *conservative* are used in a church context, as a rule of thumb insiders assume that the differences have to do with a person's operating understanding of the identity and mission of the Church. Divisions among priests, therefore, need to be examined from an ecclesiological perspective. Ecclesiologically,[9] Dulles' models offer a helpful handle for beginning to comprehend the differences that divide priests.

By way of caricature, anyone who takes the *institutional* model of Church as the exclusive understanding of what Church is would be labeled conservative; anyone who takes the *servant* model as the exclusive understanding of Church would be labeled liberal. What this looks like, again by way of caricature, might be drawn as follows. The conservative priest pastors a parish where Mass is celebrated in Latin, preceded by the rosary, followed by Benediction, and a chamber orchestra is engaged for the 10:00 A.M. high Mass on Sundays; the Baltimore catechism is taught in the school, Father appears publicly in a cassock, wears a lace alb and watered silk vestments in the sanctuary, and the parish budget is spent on education and liturgy. The liberal priest pastors a parish where the church has been whitewashed, the altar is in the middle, and the pews have no kneelers; guitars accompany the singing, the rosary and Benediction are unknown in the parish, the school is closed, the rectory has been turned into a homeless shelter at night, the parish hall provides daily meals for street people; Father appears publicly only in a sweater and open collar, he wears only a plain white alb and stole for Mass, and the lion's share of the parish budget is spent on social services.

Though the above caricatures exist, reality is far subtler among priests and people. In the main, any priest's failure to appreciate and invite a

---

[9] See ch. 5 above.

community to live out the great breadth of the Catholic tradition, and therefore his failure to integrate in community life all the ecclesiological models Dulles writes about, eventually skews the way priest and people understand Church and its ministries. No matter how genteel the priest, fundamentalism, legalism, single-issue focus, power maintenance, and lack of historical perspective all result in imbalances, with a lean toward the more conservative side of contemporary church life. Similarly, iconoclasm, ambivalence, indifference, historical relativism, and the too-eager desire to please all result in imbalances toward the liberal side. The imbalance may have to do with doctrine, moral teaching, or liturgy. Whatever its root cause, ideological posturing on the part of priests or people divides a parish, a diocese, and the Church.

A peculiarity of our time must also be noted. Sometimes a rebellious conservative looks "liberal." In this regard, a story serves best.

Melissa and Jake were both Catholic, divorced, and remarried without the benefit of annulment. Jake refused to pursue the annulment of his first marriage. Though Melissa was interested in an annulment herself, she figured there was little use since Jake was adamant on the matter. Because they had moved to a new town, however, Melissa did manage to talk Jake into seeing the parish priest about receiving Communion.

The parish priest met with each of them separately about the first marriage. He then met with them together and told them that, to his mind, each marriage could be annulled. After that declaration, he put on a stole, witnessed Melissa and Jake exchange vows and then told them they could come to Communion, with the rejoinder: "If you tell anyone I did this, I will deny it."

Conservatism might be described as offering clarity about norms and taking responsibility for enforcing them. Liberalism might be defined as inviting people to take responsibility themselves and do what they think right in their consciences. A knee-jerk reaction would be to dub this event "liberal." I would argue that that is a misnomer.

The genuinely "liberal" thing to do would have been to hear Melissa and Jake out, invite them to accept responsibility in their consciences for the judgment about the sacramentality of their first marriage, and then let them decide for themselves whether they wished to come to Communion or not. However, rather than inviting Melissa and Jake to take on personal responsibility, the priest took on the responsibility for the state of their marriage, then enforced his posture by hallowing it with a ritual gesture that had, in ecclesial legal terms, no significance whatsoever. In spite of "liberal" appearances, the priest behaved like a rebellious conservative, not a liberal.

With innumerable actions like these in our day, which seem to emerge out of deep-set anger at ecclesial authority rather than a reverence for human freedom before the overwhelming compassion of God, we experience enormous confusion about the definition of terms *liberal* and *conservative* in any given instance. This confusion itself contributes to the divisiveness among priests and within the Church as a whole.

In my experience the vast majority of priests seems to minister in the wide middle, in-between the poles. They know church norms, respect them, articulate them when asked, and generally follow them. Compassion leads many to bend them. When a divorced and remarried Protestant converts to Catholicism, for instance, many priests are content to let the conversion take priority over regularizing the marriage. If a Lutheran presents herself at the table, most priests offer her Communion. A couple may be reminded that they really ought not live together before marriage, and why, but the issue is then often dropped. The more conservative would chastise a priest for such ministry. The more liberal would wonder why he got into discussions about these matters in the first place. Though they are silent about it, most priests live and minister in the vast middle, the moderate place, in this age of massive transition in the Church. Still, ideological wars divide the ministers of unity.

### B. CONTRADICTION TEN: CALLED TO SIMPLICITY BUT LIVING IN PRIVILEGE

A priest's cash compensation—often a base salary, seniority increment, auto allowance, and sometimes stole fees (cash for Masses)—is typically between $18,000 and $31,000 a year. Priests are self-employed for Social Security tax purposes. They receive health and dental insurance, a pension, a retreat, and continuing education allowance. The parish or ministry typically provides room and board. The priest has a vacation and one day off a week. On the face of it, this compensation seems modest enough. In fact, though, most priests live a life of some privilege.

The size of a priest's cash flow means that the typical value of his compensation is in excess of $50,000 per year. For a single person in the United States that's more than merely modest. It's comfortable. Moreover, though the diocese establishes a priest's compensation, he typically controls the purse. Isn't the fox in charge of the hen house?

For instance, a committee of the presbyteral council in one Midwest diocese conducted a survey. Cash compensation in that presbytery ranges, in fact, from $19,000 to $78,000. When the priests on the high end were probed, they said that the parish thought they deserved a larger package because of the scope of their responsibilities, or the size of their salary relative to other staff, or because the parish council preferred a different compensation structure.

Another for instance. A newly arrived pastor was told by a trustee, "Father, just let me know the size of the bonus you want at Christmas, and I will take care of it with the finance committee." The pastor refused the offer. On the first All Souls Day of his tenure, the business administrator asked the pastor what he wanted done with the collection. Upon inquiry he learned that the All Souls collection each year had gone to the pastor. Research uncovered that this pastor's predecessor, during his eight-and-one-half-year tenure, skimmed about $23,000 out of the parish in bonuses and All Souls Day collections. In the parish's budget that was no big deal. For his predecessor, however, it was a Honda Accord.

All priests know stories like these and hope the bishop and the people are in the dark about them. These stories suggest that the trust bestowed upon priests in their discretionary financial power is itself a great privilege and one that too often tempts many of them to take even more privilege.

Then there's the matter of the priest's tax-free tips. Seminary canon law instructors are typically clear that priests, while they must hand over to the parish any gifts they receive because of their role, are entitled to keep gifts intended for them personally. But when discerning the intentionality, which needs to happen often enough, it is questionable who gets the benefit of the doubt. The cash gifts I receive from parishioners each year more than cover what I spend for Christmas. That is typical for most priests, and many in the church know priests who, wherever they go, manage to befriend the family who owns the car agency or has a home in Acapulco.

Though many priests live "over the store," they typically control its relative comfort. The table bell for summoning the cook to clear the dishes and bring on the next course has disappeared in most rectories, yet some priests still have a cook for at least some meals and use a parish charge card or turn in receipts for restaurant meals. Most priests are provided some housekeeping. Many have their laundry sent out. The rectory lawn is mowed, the walks are shoveled and swept, and someone else plants and weeds the flowerbeds. In the Archdiocese of St. Paul and Minneapolis, one of the nicer benefits that comes with ordination is a heated garage. Priests are not bothered with property tax assessments, household insurance bills, or household gas, water, or electricity bills. All of this is a form of privilege.

Finally, few of the people in the pews have four weeks of vacation each year, with a week of retreat and a week of continuing education above that, as priests do. Very few of them have as much control over their work and time off as the typical priest does. Nearly no one today has anything like the absolute job security priests take so for granted. Few people other than priests and bishops in our culture retire, as the priests of St. Paul and Minneapolis do, to a lovely retirement residence on prime wooded property along the Mississippi River, with three meals a day, housekeeping and laundry service—all for the low, low price of $955 per month. Most of the faithful, if they fully understood a priest's circumstances, would be green with envy.

### C. CONTRADICTION ELEVEN: MORAL AUTHORITIES IN PUBLIC BUT PRIVATELY WINKING

Priests are regarded as authorities on morals. At the same time, in the clerical culture they wink.

Priests often wink about sexual matters among themselves. For instance, two priests in a diocese, both ordained in the late forties, were widely known to be very close friends. They were seen together most everywhere and had neighboring parishes out in the rural area. Darker suspicions were confirmed when, in the mid-1970s, they started showing up at events wearing matching fur coats. The funeral of the first to die was conducted completely according to custom. But on the way out, the bishop left the procession to stop at the deceased priest's friend and extend him his personal sympathy. This public gesture looked like compassion. It was a wink.

A pastor went golfing with a fellow pastor who had a live-in housekeeper with a young son. People had long been suspicious about their relationship. After the golf game, when the two walked into the pastor's quarters, the housekeeper was sitting in the pastor's La-Z-Boy watching TV in her stocking feet. She, of course, hastily left the pastor's quarters. The pastor telling the story snickered about it. Two years later his friend left ministry and married the housekeeper. She was pregnant with their second son. Again, winking.

But priests tend to wink about more than sexual matters. In the mid-1980s, during the first wave of sexual misconduct revelations, a chancery official was overheard to remark, "You know, this sexual misconduct scandal is really awful, but wait until the folks find out about the money!" We do wink about financial matters.

The pastor whose predecessor skimmed $23,000 out of the parish told a chancery official about his findings. The official's response was, "What do you expect me to do with the information? Do you really want me to tell the boss about it?" The pastor's predecessor golfed with the bishop and occasionally had him over for dinner. He decided to let the matter go. Both priests winked.

That $19,000 to $78,000 salary range survey, which finally put on paper what the presbyteral council members all knew were years of policy violation regarding salary, was shared at the council's meeting. Several expressed some interest and concern. There were some witty exchanges. Ultimately, though, the issue was forgotten. The council winked.

Then there's the pastor who broke into tears of delighted surprise when the parish gave him a car on his twenty-fifth anniversary. Few of the parishioners at the event grasped that he had set up the parish leadership to make the gift just as he had set up the leadership at the previous parish to give him a car. Only the parochial vicar knew that the pastor had inspected the car thoroughly the night before. Winking.

Father Z. was senior associate at a midsize parish. When he retired the parish hosted a "drinks and filet under a tent" retirement party for him. It cost the parish $15,000. Father Z. himself had been on the planning committee. The pastor didn't like it but really didn't want to argue with him. More winking.

None of this is really news to most priests. Most of them could singe people's ears with winking stories. What the stories reveal the Church has lived with for decades, perhaps even centuries. The critical question is this: what is the Church supposed to do about the winking?

Three observations give some direction. First, there is a certain acceptance in the winking that feels like compassion. Perhaps priests need to consider that these warm feelings just might be counterfeit. While cold, judgmental attitudes are out of order among priests, so, too, is the failure to draw proper moral boundaries or laughing about it. Cardinal Law's form of winking was not compassion, and it served no one, not even John Goeghan and Paul Shanley.

Second, to be fair, many priests suffer from a kind of macular degeneration rather than winking. They simply fail to see the issues, or see them as pertaining to their lives. That is not to excuse them but simply to clarify reality. Third, priests' winking signals a certain decay in the clerical culture as a whole. It suggests that, at some level, the members of the culture think that their convenience is more important than the Gospel, that their discomfort about engaging one another to think again outweighs moral virtue, that sustaining the illusion of warm feelings toward one another is more critical than ill-using or scandalizing the faithful.

The rationalization that winking is kind, coupled with the instinct to avoid self-righteousness and conflict, leaves many priests still winking. The book of Proverbs reminds the Church, however: "whoever winks the eye, causes trouble."[10] Besides, the decay of the clerical culture has exploded onto the national and international stage with regard to our sexual misconduct winking at least, and to crippling effect. How much more undermining of the Gospel and the tradition are the ordained willing to withstand? How much more winking dare they do?

---

[10] Proverbs 10:10.

# Part Three:
# Considerations
# toward Transformation

# 10. Cultural Transformation

## A. A SPIRITUAL APPROACH TO TRANSFORMATION

The sexual misconduct scandal is symptomatic of a clerical culture in decay. The scandal exhibited the banality of some of our ordained ministers, their lack of integrity, deafness to the Word of God, sloth about the spiritual life, and abandonment of those with and among whom they are charged to offer a shepherd's care. It demonstrated human alienation: self-destructive dispositions, shameless exploitation, sexual predation, and a cavalier attitude to its consequences. It also manifested gross injustice, wrong order in relationships: self-preservation placed over mission, presumption, secrecy, and a warped sense of responsibility, accountability, health, and balance.

While no personal moral judgments can appropriately be made about any of the individuals involved in the scandal, a profound spiritual malaise seems to characterize the whole of it. The malaise seems grounded in faithlessness, the absence of the desire and will to search for God's presence, promise, and way—and trust God while searching and when finding—in the midst of the circumstances and relationships of daily life. Beyond faithlessness, two sets of observations about likely spiritual dispositions in these kinds of circumstances can help clarify why ordained persons would so tragically reject the spiritual ground of their vocation.

### i. Perpetrators: Sinning against Hope

All Christians are called to hope, which is the confident expectation that communion with God can be reached, both ultimately in the Kingdom and now in this life, and the commitment of one's whole life to this expectation. The commitment to celibacy is a radical personal and public proclamation that the Kingdom of God is the first commitment of the celibate, and that relationship with God, through Jesus Christ in the Holy Spirit, is so nourishing and sustaining in day-to-day human life that one can live without a spouse and children. The radical witness of celibacy is a freely chosen, profound, arduous act of hope on the part of the ordained.

The violation of celibate commitment, especially the kind of gross sexual behavior the world has seen in the most notorious cases, is a kind of hopelessness, which comprises both despair and presumption. Sexual self-indulgence leads to dejection, and dejection to a pessimistic melancholy in relationship to the goal of blessedness before God. This process leads ultimately to despair, abandonment of belief that the Kingdom and relationship with God are imaginable, much less achievable. Paul Shanley's being part owner of a motel known to provide a safe haven for promiscuous sexual encounter captures the essence of despair for a celibate priest. In presumption one recklessly or smugly relies on God to fix things when they go awry. The example of one perpetrator who took his adult female victim to a neighboring church for confession before returning her home after their sexual encounter is a striking example of presumption.

For all human beings, despair and presumption lead to a giving-up on the possibility that human relationships and societal structures can be transformed, and humanity can be reconciled to God, through prayerful human action. Loss of hope is especially devastating to the spiritual life because it leads one to withdraw altogether from the project of the Christian life. Exactly this loss of hope seems deeply etched on the faces and in the vacant eyes of Paul Shanley standing at the bar, and John Goeghan sitting at the table, of a courtroom. Looking at them it was hard to even imagine that they were once priests.[1]

Because the promise of celibacy is a profound and public act of hope, violation of it signals hopelessness: despair, presumption, or both. Because loss of hope is so fundamentally damaging to one's spirituality, a spiritual approach to the transformation of a clerical culture that has given such witness to hope's loss seems fundamentally necessary.

### ii. The Chancery: Vanity and Pride

From the mid-fourth century on, the Christian spiritual tradition has taught about the capital sins. The most ancient list enumerates eight: gluttony, lust, covetousness, anger, dejection, sloth, vanity, and pride.[2]

---

[1] I owe much of the discussion about hope to Monika K. Hellwig's "Hope" in Michael Downey, ed., *The New Dictionary of Catholic Spirituality* (Collegeville: The Liturgical Press, 1993) 506–15.

[2] Boniface Ramsey, o.p., trans. and annotator, *John Cassian: The Institutes,* Ancient Christian Writers (New York: Newman Press, 2000). See 239–52 on vainglory, 253–74 on pride.

This particular order comes from the ancient desert monks' teaching that the first six capital sins can be overcome since vanity—saying and doing things for other people's approval, pandering to the crowd—is a major motivator for conquering them. Because we would never want others to think us, for example, gluttonous, lustful, or covetous, vanity motivates us mightily to overcome these vices. But vanity's being a motivator for overcoming the first six sins means that vanity itself becomes so bloated that it can never itself be conquered. Furthermore, because we humans always struggle with vanity, we always struggle with pride, too. Consequently, both vanity and pride are pet sins for all human beings. That's why all human beings can confidently be called sinners.

Pride is a too-exaggerated desire to excel. The first of sins and the last, pride comes in two forms according to the desert monks. *Spiritual pride,* the exaggerated desire to excel in the spiritual life, assails people who are advancing in the spiritual life. It leaves them feeling puffed up in relationship with God, thinking they can attain goodness without God's protection and assistance. It is the temptation of the spiritually great. The second kind, *carnal pride,* is the trap for beginners in the spiritual life. It springs from a kind of spiritual lukewarmness: the proud never turn fully toward God. Distrusting their religious tradition, they tend to pick and choose. They hold back from the community, thinking themselves above it. They remain attached to their possessions, sharing only in a stingy way. They are puffed up about their position in the world, impatient with instruction and advice, jealous of others' success. Stuck in their opinions, they prefer to control rather than participate, to be in charge rather than cooperate.

The words and acts of many of our bishops and their chancery officials suggest vanity and pride. Like the rest of us who suffer all our days from temptations to these vices, they pandered for the approval of others—mostly in the clerical culture—held themselves above the community, remained puffed-up about their positions, and preferred to control rather than participate, to be in charge rather than cooperate. These spiritual ills of vanity and pride seem to call for, above all others, a spiritual remedy.

It is to be expected that sin, individual and systemic, would thwart our mission as a church and inhibit our transformation as well. Sin has afflicted us across the centuries and always will. Two major constellations of inhibitors, however, especially hold back the transformation of clerical culture in our time.

## B. TRANSFORMATION INHIBITOR ONE:
## THE ORGANIZATIONAL LIFE-CYCLE MORASS

The Church these days is stuck in the mud of lethargy.[3] The reasons for this state have to do with the ordinary life cycle in any organization. The Church's current stage in the organizational life cycle is one inhibitor that leaves most initiatives for change sinking into quagmire.

Fr. Richard Rohr, o.f.m., has offered around the country some helpful reflections on organizational change. He uses in some of his talks a grid, developed by the Cincinnati-based Management Design Institute, that schematizes the life cycle of an organization. It can be found in appendix 4. The theory underneath the grid is that all organizations undulate, that is, they pass through consecutively repeating life-cycle phases of breakdown and development, which follow six stages in the process of breakdown and six in the process of development.

The peak moment in an organization is a time of general consensus about its identity and mission among its primary groups. In this consensus phase of an organization's life, people trust the organization, feel that they fit and are fully invested in it. This phase is at the top of the undulating cycle.

*Operational doubt* begins the breakdown process as people in the organization start deviating from the ordinary patterns of doing things. This slippage stage, which begins to separate people into us/them relationships, is followed by *ideological doubt,* when members of the organization begin questioning its purpose and its leaders who, in a reactionary attempt to shore up the organization, offer heavily rational explanations of purpose. The members' questioning and leadership's explanations indicate a lack of integral comprehension of organizational identity and mission as well as the loss of a deep-seated sense of belonging. These developments lead to further fracture between those who rationally accept the organization's purpose and those who question it. *Ethical doubt* then sets in as people begin to understand and assert their place in the organization in terms not of its purpose but rather their personal rights: position, seniority, precedent, etc. *Absolute doubt* follows. The organization becomes polar-

---

[3] This sense of lethargy is captured perfectly in the title of Peter Steinfels' book about the ills of the Church in our time. His remedy is a new kind of leadership that will break out of trench warfare and will balance theological concern with addressing practical pastoral realities such as worship, evangelization, and fostering Catholic identity. See Peter Steinfels, *A People Adrift: The Crisis of the Roman Catholic Church in America* (New York: Simon and Schuster, 2003).

ized and lethargic. Because the organization's purpose is unclear, people act because "we've always done it this way." The organization comes to be characterized largely by empty forms. This quickly leads to *alienation,* a time when people go through the motions, feel hypersensitive in their relationships, and tend, because of their insecurity about the organization, to overreact to deviation from their own personal expectations.

When alienation drains the organization of energy, a period of *stasis* begins, which can last a very long time. It is the bottom of the undulating cycle. Visible signs of stasis include grounds poorly kept, burned out light bulbs, natty carpets, and scuffed walls. The physical space of the organization feels shabby and melancholy, which is a mirror image of the state of mind of the organization's primary groups. As stasis continues, new people in the organization typically begin to ask questions and nudge it along in particular directions. Eventually, those who are holding onto the past have insufficient energy to dismiss the new people and their energy, and so begin to give way, opening to regeneration toward a new consensus.

The *gathering* time initiates the harnessing of power for forward movement as the organization's primary groups make begrudging room for new people and allow some change to take place. As the gathering proceeds, basic *assumptions* about the organization start to shift. Anything good within the organization's possibilities is embraced as the organization explores new or renewed purpose. Success leads to acceleration of new activity. The *goals stage* follows as people and leadership together begin to analyze what they see and to make decisions about what the organization can do well and must do, and what it does less well and does not need to do. Goals are clarified, which moves the organization to *program* considerations, which, in turn, establishes the conditions and actions necessary to achieve the goals and do what the organization does best. If the thrust and program being established is an accurate response to the emerging primary group's sense of purpose, and if it is reasonably well-defined, then consensus builds about the allocation of *resources:* money, facilities, and people are invested in the new mission.

As people see what their resources can do, the *organizational structure* begins to regenerate fully. This phase in the life cycle is marked by new definition of purpose, differentiation of functions, articulation of clear lines of responsibility, and clear personal and group comprehension of respective roles within the organizational structure. This stage leads, once again, to a new peak moment in the cycle: *consensus* among the primary groups about the organization's purpose, trust in the organization, and full investment in its mission.

For example, I became pastor of a St. Paul neighborhood parish in 1993 when the parish as a whole was at stasis, the bottom of the cycle. The physical plant had about it a melancholy drabness and the people were defensive and nervous. Parish leaders told the Archdiocesan priest personnel board that they wanted the new pastor to fit in, not to bring change. The school—the tail that wagged the dog—was in ideological doubt. Its mission statement was foggy, leadership was heavy handed, the teaching staff was wary, and some parents were hostile. Everyone took an us/them stance about everyone else. The founding pastor had been in place for thirty-three years. Finally, twenty-three years after his departure, the founding consensus—the classic city neighborhood parish with a church, school, convent, playground, and not much else by way of ministry—had completely broken down.

A succession of three relatively short-term pastors did their level best to hold the organization together. Two were distinguished for their preaching. Two did some renovation projects. All three strove to be faithful to the parish community, work with their associates, proclaim the Gospel, and do pastoral ministry the best they could. Nonetheless, the organizational life patterns in the parish, because of the breakdown of the founding consensus, controlled the pastorates of all three. The breakdown took on an inexorable life of its own. The plant and grounds ran down, planning was erratic, reserves were depleted, the finance council scraped for funds, turf battles raged. In 1993, parishioners thought Holy Spirit was a large and wealthy parish with money in the bank. The facts were that it was a mid-size to small parish with a $300,000 debt, no reserves, shallow financial bench strength, and meager school and staff facilities.

After 1993, the natural organizational life process continued until the school community fell into alienation and stasis with the rest of the parish. Then renewed parishioner leadership began the process of helping the parish rise toward a new consensus about its mission. The process has been bumpy and downright painful. Nonetheless, the whole cycle of developing commitment has taken the predictable course in its own good time. The challenge of leading the parish—for staff, councils and leadership groups—has been to identify the stages of organizational life, articulate their meaning, and walk together with the community through each stage. We made many mistakes. Pushing too far too fast led to mighty resistance. The organization could not move until it was ready. Side roads diverted energy. Change created confusion and anger because some people lost long-held power. Today we have new facilities, generous stewardship, an excellent school, and a renewed sense of mission as a full-service gospel ministry parish that seeks to name, recognize, and help people use the Holy Spirit's gifts for service of the common good of the church and the world.

This story is but one in the vast constellation of organizations that comprise the Church. Every parish, every diocese, the church in the United States, the Vatican curia, and the Church universal are all somewhere on the organizational life-cycle process. Some in the Church would strongly disagree about the application of such categories to the Church. I was smugly told by one bishop, "But the Church isn't an organization!" The risen life we share in the Church is a gift of the Holy Spirit, and the Spirit blows as the Spirit will. Nevertheless I believe this organizational life-cycle understanding goes a long way toward explaining the morass the Church is in today.

Vatican II marked an immense surge of energy across the Church. It occurred in a breakdown phase of relatively empty forms and breathed excitement and life into the worldwide Church. Because of the immensity of the changes it brought, however, and people's reaction to them, a new consensus about the Church's mission in the world never took hold. Pope Paul VI's 1968 encyclical *Humanae vitae,* standing against recommendations made by papal commissions and considerable universal church opinion, and thus against what innumerable ordained and laity perceived as the spirit of the council, initiated a breakdown trajectory in the universal Church.

Consistent with this movement, and in spite of the hopeful surge his election brought to the Church, the pontificate of John Paul II has continued this trajectory in relationship to internal church life. The Pope's and the Vatican curia's seemingly punishing and heavily rational appeals for internal church order—for instance, the inquisition of theologians, ideological bend of episcopal appointments, centralization of liturgical language translation, meddling in Catholic university theology faculties, and promulgation of fussy rubrics changes—suggest that the universal Church is deep into the breakdown process. Moreover, Pope John Paul's age and physical health have the Church at the breakdown phase of his pontificate as well. Though some national churches are certainly exceptions, patterns suggest that the Church universal is struggling between ideological and ethical doubt; that is what our current morass seems to indicate.

The church in the United States seems to be even farther along in the cycle than the Church universal. The double messages bishops offered perpetrators of sexual misconduct, the lack of clear and resounding voices during the scandal, the sense that bishops were being led, either by the Vatican or by lawyers, rather than leading—all of these situations suggest a kind of paralysis in the American church.

The organizational life-cycle movement is as natural on the national and international stage as it is on the local. It has always existed, which is why the history of the Church looks as it does. It will always exist. The current stage of breakdown, wherever we are within it—arguably stasis for the U.S. church and at ethical doubt for the universal Church—will proceed toward development of a new consensus as the years and decades pass. The challenge of leading in these years will be for the Church's primary groups to identify the stages of organizational life, articulate their meaning, and walk with the Church through them. Pushing too far too fast will surface resistance. The Church cannot move until it is ready. Side roads will divert energy. Still transformation will come.

I note the current morass and offer a perspective on it not only to suggest a possible explanation for it, but also to make the point that those of us who want transformation cannot expect much right now. The glacial pace of ecclesiastical change is legend. Our current state adds to the likelihood that the transformation many of us seek is not around the corner.

Accurately naming the phase in the cycle can empower us to help lead within it, as well as prepare ourselves for the next phase of the movement when the time is ripe. The Benedictines in liturgy, the Germans in doctrinal theology, the French in ecclesiology, and the Americans in the area of religious liberty did massive and brilliant work long before Vatican II, preparing the Church for that transformation moment. Those who became council luminaries generally suffered beforehand for their work, but when the time came they were ready. Their work was of such integrity that bishops with limited understanding themselves found it compelling, trusted it enough to use it in the council documents and thereby set the Church—briefly, and yet to come—on a renewed trajectory.

In the midst of the current morass, our task is to prepare for the work of cultural transformation. Preparation demands that we bring new ideas, new ways of relating and new material reality to the table within and for the Church. It means that we must do some experimenting, some "pushing the envelope" in our daily lives and in the life of our faith communities. Our progress now will likely be modest and misunderstood. Nonetheless, history suggests that if we trust in the Holy Spirit we shall not be disappointed.

## C. TRANSFORMATION INHIBITOR TWO:
## THE ELEPHANTS IN THE ROOM

What the twelve-step movement calls "the elephants in the room" stand in the way of change. In the midst of the morass, five elephants in particular sit in the middle of the room of cultural transformation inhibiting it by blocking the view and movement forward. They need to be named if we are to remain healthy and realistic about what's possible. Naming them might assist us in focusing what transformation can and should be about now and in the long run. It should make us better able to assess when to move and on what front in bringing about cultural transformation. The elephants are formidable: the Vatican, the bishops, the seminary, and the ordination questions regarding married priests and women priests.

### i. The Vatican[4]

The pope is bishop of Rome, absolute monarch of the 108.7-acre Vatican City and head of the Roman Catholic Church in both its Eastern and Western dispensations.[5] The Vatican is an ancient seat of government in which the monarch is surrounded by a curia (court) of a few thousand functionaries who keep the machinery of governing a worldwide institution well-oiled. Though the Vatican exists for otherworldly reasons, everything one would expect from a seat of government is elemental to it, including high purpose and corruption, altruism and ambition, collegial cooperation and struggles for control. As an institution with a singular and complex mission, as well as centuries of experience, its sophistication and subtlety are unparalleled. To better serve its mission and improve its chances of being understood in the world and by the Church, the Vatican is a secretive organization of mazelike operation that as vigorously protects its rights as it exercises its responsibilities. Its essential mission is to oversee the proclamation of the Gospel to the

---

[4] For a very helpful and detailed account of what the Vatican is and how it works, see Thomas J. Reese, *Inside the Vatican: The Politics and Organization of the Catholic Church* (Cambridge, Mass.: Harvard University Press, 1996).

[5] The Eastern Church includes twenty-one relatively self-governing churches in communion with the Holy See. Arising out of the political circumstances of the ancient Roman Empire as well as disputes over doctrine across the centuries, these churches have emerged out of five traditions and have their own liturgical rite for celebrating the Eucharist. Depending upon how one regards the 1990s permission to use the Tridentine rite, the Western Church comprises three rites for celebrating Eucharist (four if the Tridentine is included—though that makes two Latin rites and is rather inconsistent and confusing). The Latin Rite is by far the largest of all the rites, and the one to which the popes have typically belonged.

world. Its methods are as simple or as complex as they need to be to accomplish its mission in the multi-layered political, social, economic, and cultural circumstances within and across the nations of the world.

We ordinary mortals have little power and no toehold to change the culture of an organization so ancient and complex as the Vatican, staffed by such highly educated, diplomatically trained, and deeply committed personnel, who have such broad, diverse, distinctive, and nuanced global relationships, political finesse, and ready access to peasants and potentates. Even those within the Vatican are limited in their ability to effect change in a place caught in the paradox that the bureaucracy is entrenched and the winds of the Spirit blow where they will. This point is illustrated well by considering the elections of Pope Paul VI and Pope Benedict XV.

Upon his election, Pope Paul VI was severely hemmed in by circumstances. He faced significant opposition from cardinals suspicious of the direction he would give to the remaining sessions of Vatican II. Of the eighty-one cardinal electors, some twenty-two to twenty-five refused to vote for him "even when his election was assured . . . They were mostly Italian, and mostly the Curia. Their refusal to vote for him meant that they were not prepared to yield an inch."[6] On the other side he "had another, more pressing problem: he was not John XXIII."[7] Paul VI knew that his reign would be in continuity with Pope John XXIII, that he had made significant contributions to organizing the council when John XXIII could not,[8] and that he was well-qualified to bring the council to a beneficial conclusion. He also knew that Pope John XXIII was beloved and popular while he was not likely to be, that John XXIII had the reputation of being a "liberal" when he was really more conservative, more traditional, and that the expectations roused by John XXIII would leave Paul VI's pontificate unappreciated. This strain from all sides characterized Paul VI's whole reign and, coupled with the response to the encyclical *Humanae vitae,* continues to cloud over his remarkable pontificate.[9] Clearly even popes have limited control over what's cooking in the Vatican kitchens or how their actions will be received or understood.

---

[6] Peter Hebblethwaite, *Paul VI* (New York: Paulist Press, 1993) 331.

[7] Ibid., 339. See 339 and 340 for a full treatment of Paul VI's reflections on the problem.

[8] Ibid. See 304–08.

[9] In a piece of unpublished correspondence of June 3, 2003, Fr. Theodore Hesburgh, C.S.C., writes: "It is not easy to explain how the Council did so much more than was expected of it. I give that credit to the Holy Spirit, some intrepid theologians who paved new paths, and the total dedication of Paul VI to position the Church much better in the modern world."

A story about Pope Benedict XV's election makes a different point. Rafael Cardinal Merry Del Val was secretary of state throughout the reign of Pope Pius X at the beginning of the twentieth century. An archbishop at thirty-five and a cardinal at thirty-eight, Merry Del Val was a stately, patrician, and subtle diplomat known for his rigidity. His undersecretary of state was Giacomo Della Chiesa. Though the highly educated, noble, and punctilious Della Chiesa had a good relationship with Pius X, Merry Del Val mistrusted the thin little man with the limp, hump back, and one eye and ear noticeably higher than the other because he was ever-tactful, yet never truly zealous in carrying out Merry Del Val's concerns. When the see of Bologna fell vacant, an archdiocese bristling with difficulties, Della Chiesa was sent there to be its archbishop. Ordinarily a cardinalatial see, Della Chiesa sat for seven years without a red hat.[10]

It is the role of the secretary of state to present the pope with a list of candidates to be named cardinal. The pope then approves, cardinals are named, and a consistory is held. Because of his antipathy toward Della Chiesa, Merry Del Val kept his name off successive lists. Pius X eventually grasped what was happening, put Della Chiesa's name on the list, and made him a cardinal in 1914.[11] Three months later Pius X died. In the conclave that followed, Della Chiesa was elected Pope Benedict XV.

Immediately following the election, when Cardinal Merry Del Val approached the new pope in the line of cardinals who came forward to make their personal obedience to him, Benedict XV leaned down to the cardinal and said to him, "The stone which the builders rejected has become the cornerstone."[12]

Merry Del Val responded with heavy irony, "And it is remarkable in our eyes!" Then he kissed the new pope's ring.[13] Merry Del Val was replaced as secretary of state and lost influence at the Vatican until his death in 1930 at age sixty-five.[14]

---

[10] See Walter H. Peters, *The Life of Benedict XV* (Milwaukee: Bruce Publishing, 1959) 67–69.

[11] Ibid., 68.

[12] Psalm 118:22-23 reads:

> "The stone that the builders rejected
>    has become the chief cornerstone.
> This is the Lord's doing;
>    It is marvelous in our eyes."

[13] This story is found in Peters, op. cit., 284, n. 40. Peters suggests that it is likely a wags tale invented "with the Roman student's genius for caricature." Nonetheless, it captures the essence of Merry Del Val's and Della Chiesa's strained relationship.

[14] See John F. Pollard, *The Unknown Pope: Benedict XV (1914–1927) and the Pursuit of Peace* (New York: Geoffrey Chapman, 2000) 59–68, for the conclave story and Pollard's reportage

The facts surrounding the election of Paul VI and the continuing circulation of the stories surrounding that of Benedict XV speak volumes about the high art of Vatican politics, the Vatican's acute sensitivities, and the ease with which its functionaries, even under a pope's nose, accomplish their idiosyncratic ends. These also speak as well of the Holy Spirit's remarkable and unpredictable work in the Church whatever its functionaries might intend.[15]

In sum, the popes are limited by circumstances at the Vatican. If an Italian curial insider like Pope Paul VI can be adamantly opposed, imagine how in the dark a Polish outsider or how long it would take a new pope to become genuinely "in charge." Even popes are able to control and shape the Vatican only to a certain extent, depending on their priorities, their administrative abilities, the effectiveness of their appointments, the clarity of their communication, their predecessor, and the faithful's openness to them. Still, the wind of the Spirit blows as it will. The Vatican is a very large elephant in the room over which our only control is to make publicly known what we think appropriate, and then most fervently pray.

### ii. The Bishops

Much the same conclusion might be reached about the bishops of the United States. That is certainly what the work of Fr. Tomas Reese, s.j., would suggest. Though some bishops have retired and others appointed since their publication, his books about the archbishops of the United States and the workings of the United States Catholic Conference offer an illuminating picture of our American bishops.[16]

---

of how difficult it must have been for the Merry Del Val clique to lose election as well as for Merry Del Val to be relegated to an insignificant post.

[15] The Della Chiesa story brings to mind that, after twenty-four years in the secretariat of state, ten as prosecretary, Giovanni Battista Montini was suddenly appointed archbishop of Milan. Although traditionally a cardinalatial see, Milan's Archbishop Montini spent four years without a red hat. The first cardinal made by the newly elected Pope John XXIII in 1958 was Montini. Pope John is said to have quipped, "If Montini had been cardinal, Roncalli would not be Pope." In consideration of the likely political disfavor with Pius XII into which Montini fell, the picture of his arrival in Milan, in the rain, on his knees kissing the ground, is especially pointed. See Peter Hebblethwaite, *Paul VI*, 278–79, for a reflection on Pius XII's disfavor. See William E. Barrett, *Shepherd of Mankind: A Biography of Pope Paul VI* (Garden City, N.Y.: Doubleday & Co., 1964) plate 16, for the picture.

[16] Thomas J. Reese, s.j., *Archbishop: Inside the Power Structure of the American Catholic Church* (San Francisco: Harper and Row, 1989). I am assuming that the information Reese has compiled for the archbishops is about the same as that of the rest of the bishops; in fact, the archbishops are probably younger upon their first appointment than those who remain bishops. Thomas J. Reese, s.j., *A Flock of Shepherds: The National Conference of Catholic Bishops* (Kansas

Who are our bishops? They are largely middle-aged and older white males[17] who come from Catholic neighborhoods and had a Catholic education. They mostly began their seminary career in high school and are priests known for their prudence, stability, adaptability, and generally nonauthoritative style. They were selected to be pastoral leaders because they were brighter, harder working, and more loyal to the Church and to their bishop than many of their peers. Chosen through an extended, secret process,[18] particular priests become bishops because they value teamwork, respect for their colleagues, and a sense of tradition. They consequently tend as a group to place priority on unity and charity over efficiency and effectiveness. They are more reactive than initiating and forward thinking, more oriented toward a siege mentality than honest debate. Liberal versus conservative among the bishops typically means merely that some have greater and some lesser tolerance for doctrinal and disciplinary variance; they diverge from each other in emphasis, not substance.[19] Bishops who have the ear of the pope dominate the bishop selection process; the laity of the church are seldom consulted. Enormous, anxious care is taken in the selection of bishops because once they are in place they are nigh impossible to remove.

These facts suggest why the U.S. church saw no luminaries among the bishops during the 2002 sexual misconduct scandal. Archbishop Rembert Weakland, a brilliant, well-respected and independent-minded spokesman for liberal concerns, lost credibility because of his payoff to a victim. Cardinals Edward Eagan of New York and Theodore McCarrick of Washington, D.C., were too new to their posts to provide effective voice or leadership. Eagan was also tainted by the compromises unearthed about his tenure at Bridgeport. Cardinal Mahony of Los Angeles came mildly to the fore, but his teflon image was scratched mightily when the dedication of his $189,000,000 cathedral coincided with the massive layoff of archdiocesan staff because of fund shortages. For all his depth and brilliance, Cardinal Francis George of Chicago has too narrow an appeal; Bishop Kenneth Untener of Saginaw, Auxiliary Bishop

---

City: Sheed and Ward, 1992). For a perspective on the effectiveness of the state Catholic conferences, see David Yamane, "The Bishops and Politics: Has the scandal stilled the church's voice? Don't believe it," *Commonweal* (vol. CXXX, no. 10, May 23, 2003) 17–20.

[17] Reese, *Flock of Shepherds*, 66. In 1989 they were appointed at age forty-nine on average. Today they would likely be appointed as a slightly older age on average. Then they were 84 percent white.

[18] See ibid., 5–17, and Reese, *Archbishop*, 1–52.

[19] Reese, *Flock of Shepherds*, 15.

Thomas Gumbleton of Detroit, and Archbishop Harry Flynn of St. Paul and Minneapolis have too small a platform and are less than aggressive about seizing the spotlight. Though he was articulate in interviews, Bishop Wilton Gregory, the bishops' conference president, conveyed mixed messages as he told the bishops in one speech that "we are the ones" responsible for the significant elements of the sexual misconduct scandal, and in another that sinister forces were trying to take advantage of the scandal to weaken the Church. These among the bishops are the very well-known; none of them offered a consistent or compelling message to the national Church.[20]

During the scandal and its aftermath, the performance of the bishops' conference as a whole was and remains disappointing. While content to articulate unprecedented sanctions against priests, the conference's failure to publicly rebuke bishops who have perpetrated gross injustice against the faithful seems especially reprehensible. Though bishops are rumored to be angry with others in the conference, the body of bishops publicly passes off the responsibility for public rebuke to the Vatican and washes its hands of it. To be fair to them, however, their failure may indicate that the bishops were unsure about where to begin and where to end in offering rebuke since numerous cases continued to surface in dioceses across the United States.

Throughout the most intense period of scandal, it was also unclear who cares pastorally for the bishops. Many of them live alone. They work in a clubby atmosphere, surrounded by people chosen to do their bidding, some of whom are ambitious to become their auxiliary or their replacement. This leaves most bishops relatively isolated. They spend huge blocks of time glad-handing people they can never get to know well, albeit with a shepherd's care. Many are workaholics who are unsure of their friends, defensive around their enemies, concerned about the Church as a whole, but largely standing alone. The ever-increasing centralizing tendency of the Vatican leaves bishops seeming more and more like branch managers of the central corporation in Rome rather than pastors in their own right. They are subject to the same kind of political maneuvering, jockeying for reward, and suffering of indignity that the nation has come to see in the corporate scandals. Most all of the bishops

---

[20] Two other bishops who have potential on the national scene are Archbishop Michael Sheehan of Santa Fe, who took over for Bishop O'Brien when he resigned his see at Phoenix after a hit and run accident, and Archbishop Sean Patrick O'Malley of Boston. It would seem, however, that these men likely will be more focused on their huge diocesan responsibilities rather than the national scene.

are personally pressed—enormously so—from all sides, likely finding personal support mostly from one another.

Because the air is thin at their heights, bishops can be out of touch with real life as well. If their retirement package includes a car, office, secretary, residence, meals, housekeeping, travel, and $1,900 per month, imagine their resources in office! Two stories illustrate the point.

A priest flew with two bishops to a funeral of a third. The priest attended because the bishop had been his predecessor as pastor. In their conversation together the bishops lamented that priests were not attending; the bishops thought their nonattendance sad and even reprehensible. The priest had to remind them that it was holy week, an impossible time for most priests to get away. Moreover, neither bishop had any idea that the airplane flight cost $800.

The second story. A bishop was very pleased to share how he got an addition onto his suburban home just before his retirement. He invited two old friends, one an architect and the other a contractor, with their wives, to a cookout. During the gathering he told them that he wanted a 20 x 20 foot great room added onto the house, "And, of course," he said with self-satisfied twinkle in his eye and a chuckle, "I told them. 'I want it to cost nothing.'"

The men complied. The addition, which the bishop intended to use for hospitality, cost him practically nothing. "The Sacred Heart hangs over the fireplace," he said with delight. "You open doors on one side of the room, and there is the tabernacle for prayer and adoration. You close that, and open doors on the other side of the room, and there's the wet bar." One is reminded of the old saw in the clerical culture: Jesus came proclaiming the Kingdom of God . . . and all he got was the Church.

A longtime observer of many bishops on the national and international scene used to make two snide observations about bishops. One was that the miter was not a hat but a large candlesnuffer; when the miter went on, the lights went out. The other was that ordination to the episcopacy brought with it a darkening of the intellect and concomitant strengthening of the will. These observations have less to do with the bishops' gifts, motives, or intelligence than they do with their often being out of touch with real life.

The Vatican tightly controls bishop selection, and bishops cooperate in that fully. Many bishops are inclined to be seen as stalwarts of orthodoxy, even while they are committed to keeping peace. The peer pressure among the bishops as a group, especially for those who wish to get ahead, is enormous and silencing. Many lead a lonely life. All are caught between Rome above and their priests and people below. Some of the bishops are out of touch. These factors leave the bishops disinclined toward change.

### iii. The Seminary

The seminary has a pivotal role in shaping the contours of clerical culture at any given moment in our history. How the seminary fulfills its mission shapes the church of a diocese or a nation for generations. The seminary is in the bishop's complete control, and he keeps one eye on the Vatican for guidance.[21] This shape of things leaves the seminary off-limits to intervention by any but the episcopal leaders of the clerical culture and the highly circumscribed seminary rectors and lay people admitted to seminary boards of trustees. The seminary is a large elephant.

The best current work on seminaries in the United States offers a balanced assessment of their strengths and weaknesses.[22] Over the last ten years, management has improved because boards and administrators are more experienced. Programs are more sensitive to personal growth and celibacy formation for the seminarians as well as to the multi-cultural reality of both the U.S. church and contemporary students. Seminaries have improved their facilities and technological resources. At the same time, the multicultural programs and faculty are not yet adequate for the complexity of cultures that comprise the U.S. church.[23] Ecumenism is largely ignored in seminary curricula. Collaboration is "neither clearly understood nor widely practiced in theologates or in the church more broadly."[24] Recruitment of seminary students can lead to accepting students whose aptitude for ministry is lower than is necessary. Funds and formation programs are inadequate for lay ministry students. Technology is insufficiently integrated into the seminary faculty's approach to teaching. Ideological dispute divides some faculties. Program planning and evaluation in seminaries, especially in light of their broad responsibilities, needs more careful attention, especially in the area of reaching students intellectually and in their human, spiritual, and pastoral formation.

To this expert assessment, based on extensive interviews in forty-four institutions across the country, I would add but two observations.

---

[21] See ch. 6 above.

[22] Katerina Schuth, *Seminaries, Theologates, and the Future of Church Ministry: An Analysis of Trends and Transitions* (Collegeville: The Liturgical Press, 1999).

[23] See the essay on the larger cultural issues by R. Scott Appleby in ibid., especially 1–23.

[24] Ibid., 237.

First, it would be extremely helpful if the bishops could come to common agreement about the fundamental role toward which they want the seminary to educate and form seminarians. I spent in excess of thirteen years in the seminary, and another seven years engaged on seminary formation staff. Throughout this score of years the fundamental discernment question was: do I want to become a priest, do I have the call and the aptitudes to be a priest? This question leads one to consider celibacy closely as well as to reflect on preaching the word, presiding at sacraments, offering catechesis across all ages, and attending to the sick and those in need. Phrased in this way, the question dominated my own years of discernment as well as those during which I assisted others to discern. Only after leaving seminary work, ten years after ordination, did I realize that, like so many before me, I was asking only part of the question. I neglected to ask: do I want to become a pastor, do I have the skills and feel the call to be a pastor?

Being a pastor requires an array of leadership skills: from helping a community come to a vision of its mission to making sure the revenue stream keeps flowing, from ordering the parish's gospel ministries to negotiating with the contractor about the boiler system, from calling the community to work for justice in the neighborhood and the city to clarifying property rights with the neighbor and his attorneys or terminating a consistently insubordinate employee. These circumstances, which dominate a pastor's day-to-day existence and create challenges and stress no less than exhilaration and deep satisfaction, are largely passed over in seminary formation. That is understandable: few bishops, seminary administrators, or seminary faculty have ever been pastors. Yet, for instance, about 165 of the just over 237 diocesan priests active in the Archdiocese of St. Paul and Minneapolis are pastors. They have been little prepared by the seminary for community leadership and the matters that daily will preoccupy them.

The answer to the question about being a priest can be very different from that about being a pastor. A follower with mild social competence, poor supervisory skills, theological quirks, saccharine piety, no facility for leading a meeting, and little instinct for community tone can emerge through the large-weave sieve of the first question. He would most likely be caught in the small-weave sieve of the second. The church of the United States has a far greater shortage of good pastors than it has a shortage of priests. Only the large sieve question, however, is solidly in place among the bishops and across the seminaries.

The consequence of focus on only one discernment question for ordination candidates is that bishops and seminary faculties, not to mention students, are oriented toward a relatively narrow institutional and sacramental understanding of ordained ministry rather than a fuller, broader, and more realistic view. Were the bishops to seriously advise seminarians and seminaries that the pastoring question is as important as the priesthood question, then the call to ordained ministry would have greater appeal in itself and would likely attract people who want to lead. Seminary education and formation would grow closer to the real experience of pastors and people. The church would also ordain higher quality candidates.

The second observation has to do with the contextual shape of the seminary program. I recently stopped by the city religious goods store and noticed a cassock and surplice in the display window. I asked the manager about it. "That's what they want, Father. The seminarians are buying cassocks, and surplices, too. Lacey ones!" This window display and the reason for it is symptomatic of a seminary hothouse environment out of touch with the people, the parish, and the vast middle that is American parish life. The seminary program needs to be reoriented.

The four years of community living in preparation for parish priesthood has little about it that connects to what the priest experiences in a lifetime of living alone or with one other priest in a parish house. Community living is a high value. Seminarians need to have an experience of it to understand Christian community in a parish. It is also the only way even to begin to comprehend certain elements of ecclesial life: the Liturgy of the Hours, focused growth in the spiritual life, and the strong support that is possible among others who share a common calling. Besides, conversations happen among students and staff in community life that are impossible in other settings.

At the same time, however, living in a parish is also a high value. A seminarian needs to see what the daily life of a priest is like over the long haul: its joys, its loneliness, and the creativity and adjustments it demands. He needs to grapple with the endless calls for ministry and the hard work it takes to live in personal balance in the midst of those calls. The seminarian needs to see, share in, and talk about the very practical, concrete realities of meetings, doorbells, parish staff, finances, whining parents, doting seniors, late nights, early mornings, and the rectory standing immediately adjacent to the parking lot and playground.

A healthier and more realistic model of seminary formation would be more balanced between community and parish life. For instance, two years in intense community formation and course work, on the model of a religious order novitiate, should be adequate time for four-year students.[25] Then following the community experience, seminarians ought to be placed in parish rectory living, with continuing seminary course work and some community gatherings being part of that experience. This kind of balance would help relieve the hothouse atmosphere of seminary study—whether that leads to the purchase of cassocks and surplices or the avoidance of clerical dress altogether—and offer seminarians a more realistic view of the church for which they are being ordained. Greater experience of parish life, coupled with attentive mentoring, is key to seminary formation in our time and a necessary balance to community formation.

In the end, however, the responsibility for the seminary belongs to the bishops, who look to the Vatican for direction and support. This elephant we can do relatively little to address.

### iv. The Ordination Questions

The ordination of women as well as married priests are mammoth concerns that rear up constantly in the media whenever controversy arises about the ordained, particularly controversy with a sexual subtext. The questions are very different.

Whether ordained ministers are married or unmarried is a question of church discipline, not doctrine. We have both in all rites East and West. The radical witness to the transcendence of the Kingdom, and to God's love as enough for a human being's abiding satisfaction and deep completion, makes celibacy an invaluable witness to the Church and the world, especially in sexually preoccupied cultures. Certainly the witness of faithful marriage among ordained ministers is similarly valuable in cultures where marriage is undervalued and permanence is regarded lightly. The witness is simply different, and church leaders need to assess the relative value of either form of witness from the perspective of two thousand years of church history as well as the impact the Church wishes to have in cultures across the globe.

The current posture among our leaders seems more reactive than forward thinking, yet, in the end, they may very well be right in upholding celibacy as a Latin Rite discipline. In light of a man's freedom to choose

---

[25] Pre-theology students would need their time of study—one year or two—to be in community life. These years would be over and above the first two years of theologate study in a community context.

or not choose ordained ministry, and the apparent lack of universal consensus about changing the discipline of celibacy, this elephant requires little comment. It is the topic of discussion for Uncle Herbert and Aunt Gertrude every time I sit down at a wedding banquet or funeral luncheon. There is no end in sight to contemporary, wide-ranging discussion. Consensus will emerge eventually.

The ordination of women is a much more difficult question. Many argue that the question is also a matter of discipline, not doctrine. Pope John Paul II, however, shifted the ground under everyone's feet some years ago when he asserted that the ordination of men is "from the Lord," not merely a disciplinary question. His assertion alone takes the question out of the realm of discussion and consensus and places it in the realm of theological debate with high nuance. Is the ordination of men from the Lord, or no? How do we make that judgment? If the pope has said it is, has theologian Wojtyla opined or has Pope John Paul II taught? What are the implications for papal authority in either case? For as painful a question as women's ordination is for legions of people across the country and the world, this very heavy elephant is here to stay and be discussed, debated, and probably misunderstood—in spite of papal protests or because of them—for a long time to come.

## D. WHAT WILL BE CONSIDERED

Transformation of the clerical culture is a political and a spiritual enterprise. Though mindful of the significant political skills required to effect change because of the spiritual malaise that the sexual misconduct scandal has exposed, what follows is essentially a spiritual approach to cultural transformation. It is largely oriented toward the ordained themselves since they are the primary actors who will need to lead clerical cultural change. The mere articulating of the clerical culture background, contradictions, and possible transforming remedies, however, makes the ordained accountable to the laity of the Church, who have every right and duty to hold their priests responsible for their faithful and hopeful, their holy, loving, and just community leadership. It is precisely in the dialogue about what ordained leadership is and ought to be that ordained and lay can come together and begin transformation of the clerical culture and the whole of the Church.

# 11. Being Leaders in Holiness

## A. TENDERS OF THE ASSEMBLY'S INTEGRITY

Priests preside in the Eucharist. That role profoundly shapes how others perceive the priest and how the priest perceives himself. Traditionally, particularly in the best priestly spiritualities offered across the ages,[1] the role of presiding at the Eucharist calls priests to mirror its meaning in all they are, say and do. Why?

In *Ancient Israel's Faith and History*,[2] George Mendenhall demonstrates that the Eucharist, the new covenant in Christ's blood,[3] is an ancient form of oath.[4] The Eucharist is not a spoken oath, Mendenhall argues, but an enacted oath. In the Eucharist those who eat and drink the body and blood of the Lord swear personal allegiance to Jesus Christ and swear that they will embody Jesus Christ in the whole of their lives. Flowing from the Eucharist, the Christian way of life is not an external matter of rules. Rather, it is an embodied, enacted covenant relationship that links God's reign to human integrity.[5]

The practical import of Mendenhall's thesis is that everyone gathered in the eucharistic assembly holds his or her whole self in his or her hands before God in the oath-taking that is the Eucharist.[6] The priest's role as presider intensifies the seriousness of the oath-taking for the priest. Because the priest leads the eucharistic assembly, his personal integrity has

---

[1] See ch. 4 above.

[2] George Mendenhall, ed. Gary Herion, *Ancient Israel's Faith and History: An Introduction to the Bible in Context* (Louisville: Westminster John Knox Press, 2001) 226–29.

[3] 1 Corinthians 11:25; Luke 22:20.

[4] Mendenhall, op cit., 226.

[5] Ibid., 235.

[6] In Robert Bolt's play, *A Man for All Seasons*, Thomas More, who dies rather than swear an oath falsely, says to his daughter Margaret, "When a man takes an oath, Meg, he's holding his own self in his own hands. Like water. And if he opens his fingers *then*—he needn't hope to find himself again." Robert Bolt, *A Man for All Seasons* (New York: Vintage Books, 1962) 81.

a direct impact on the Christian mission. The Church saw this fact dramatically demonstrated in 2002 when the integrity and credibility of its mission was damaged because priests and bishops had compromised their own integrity and the community's by abusing their power.

Just like for everyone who shares in the Eucharist, the priest's integrity as disciple of the Lord Jesus is a sacred trust that must be tended. Presidency in the assembly, however, places the priest in the position of being tender also of the assembly's integrity as the community of disciples. Consequently, the priest's being what the Eucharist proclaims him as presider to be is a ringing mandate and weighty responsibility that, like it or not, grounds priestly leadership and has a real impact on the Church's mission.

## B. TENDERS OF THE WORD

In *The Changing Face of the Priesthood,* Donald Cozzens rightly calls tending the word "the core of a priest's spirituality."[7] He quite appropriately focuses tending the word on preparing for preaching. According to the decrees of the Second Vatican Council[8] and the Code of Canon Law,[9] proclaiming the Word of God is the first responsibility of the priest. This ministry, done well, is by far a priest's most demanding responsibility. It is far less a ministry of teaching than of inspiring, and it calls the preacher to give himself over in a profound way to God in prayer and in a focused way to the inspiration offered by God throughout any given day.

### i. Sunday Preaching

Proclaiming the Word on Sundays, when the community of faith assembles for the weekly celebration of the resurrection of the Lord, needs to be the first priority of the ministry of priests, especially pastors. At its best, preaching well on Sunday is a weeklong process. It requires that the preacher begin his preparation by praying the next Sunday's readings throughout the week, usually beginning on the previous Sunday evening or Monday. The aim of this prayer is to open to the word of the texts in the juxtaposition in which they are offered, and then to the

---

[7] Donald Cozzens, *The Changing Face of the Priesthood* (Collegeville: The Liturgical Press, 2000) 85. See 83–94.

[8] Austin Flannery, o.p., ed., *Vatican Council II: The Conciliar and Post Conciliar Documents,* rev. ed. (Northport, N.Y.: Costello Publishing, 1992) 868.

[9] *Code of Canon Law* (Washington, D.C.: Canon Law Society of America, 1983) 287–91, especially canon 762.

themes of the liturgical season, current events, the assembly's need, and one's own spiritual hunger. Within the first couple of days of praying with the texts, the preacher typically develops a sense of subject and direction for the next Sunday's homily.

A three-layered process then draws out this developing sense further. With the help of Scripture commentaries, one layer is studying the text for its own depths of meaning. Does the text affirm the preacher's own sense of the fundamental subject or direction? Modify it? Reshape it? Inform it? A second layer is attentive listening all week long to the radio, reading materials, people's thoughts and feelings, and the promptings of one's own heart. This attentive listening to all around and within one's self also expands and deepens the original direction of a homily, shapes its contours, and offers story, perspective, and language. The third layer of the process is the composing of the homily. For some preachers this is more structured, for others less. Nonetheless every homily requires time and energy, either in a focused mental process or in rewrite after rewrite after rewrite, to give it structure and balance and to tune it finely for delivery, mindful of the experience of the whole Sunday assembly in the Eucharist.

This great care must be taken in the preaching, the homilist offering the very deepest and broadest of his own spiritual reflection, because the homily is an extension of the Word of God and, within the Eucharist, itself the Word of God.

### ii. Weekday Preaching

Daily Mass preaching is, typically, offered in a form called the *postil,* a two- or three-minute reflection intended to focus the assembly's mind and heart by highlighting a particular point for their prayerful consideration. Preparation for the postil requires an abbreviated version of the process described above. It includes praying the readings until a subject or direction emerges, consulting Scripture commentaries, attentive reflecting on one's own experience and the assembly's, and composition. It usually includes pondering the readings through the prism of the seasons of the liturgical year, like Advent or Lent, or, often enough, the life of a particular saint (the Japanese martyrs, for instance) or event in the history of the tradition (the Battle of Lepanto under the commemoration of Our Lady of the Rosary).

While the emphasis of Sunday preaching is on the integration of many factors in the world, the Church, the preacher's life, and the week, weekday preaching tends to push the preacher to fathom ever more honestly and rigorously his own spiritual depths. The priest's daily closeness to the Scripture texts, the often discordant juxtaposition of the texts offered on a given day, and the difficulty of bringing the word home day after day into the lives of the people with whom the preacher is celebrating are all profoundly molding experiences for the preacher. The repetitiousness of this process over the years, the rigor of the discipline it requires, and the striving to remain creative and provocative confront the careful preacher in ways both painful and thrilling, offering ever-deeper insight into the message of Jesus and his call to discipleship. The commitment to integrity will drive the daily preacher to a confrontation with the hard reality of his faults and to a wrenching personal call to change and conversion.

In its own way, though it is far less carefully scrutinized, daily preaching is more demanding of the spiritual life and the integrity of the priest than Sunday preaching. Daily Mass preaching, more than Sunday preaching, changes a priest's life with the passing decades if only because of its insistent press upon the priest's focus and time.

### iii. Special Occasion Preaching

As if the above were not enough, most priests also face the need to preach funerals or weddings during any given week, sometimes multiples of one or the other. This preaching, too, places personal and spiritual demands.

For each of these occasions the family or couple being married usually selects the readings, giving the preacher an opportunity to ask them why they selected the particular Scripture texts and how they understand their meaning. This dialogue is a critical element of the homily preparation for funerals and weddings because the life situation of particular persons is the lens through which the occasion and the Scriptures are interpreted. That is to say, the deceased or the couple usually provides the story through which the whole assembly, in the preaching, is invited to reflect upon the Word of God. Marian's having spent a lifetime of feeling unloved and making everyone else miserable, or a couple's meeting on a fishing expedition, are the often brilliant prisms through which the Word of God can be proclaimed to an assembly in a uniquely compelling way.

These occasions for preaching require of the priest the same prayer and study with the texts he would do for Sundays and weekdays. They add to the process the priest's need to ponder the lives of particular human beings and weave their lives and the pondering into the fabric of the texts and the message that flows from them. At its very best, preaching for these occasions offers singular grace to the preacher and the assembly gathered.

### iv. Spiritual Proclamation of the Word

In the beginning of the book of Genesis, when God speaks creation comes into being. The Word of God has a dynamic, creative power and energy that, in itself, shapes reality and gives life.[10] This same life-bearing Word pitched his tent among us,[11] ultimately leaving behind for us his dynamic, creative, life-giving word:

> Indeed, the Word of God is living and active, sharper than any two-edged sword, piercing until it divides soul from spirit, joints from marrow; it is able to judge the thoughts and intentions of the heart.[12]

This is the Word we proclaim in the Sacred Scriptures at Mass during the Liturgy of the Word, and, by extension, in the Eucharistic Prayer. Because of the dynamic power of the Word of God, all those proclaiming it, particularly the priest as he proclaims the Gospel and the Eucharistic Prayer, need to do it with careful attention to the text's power to change minds and hearts in the proclamation. The process of preparing for proclaiming the Word of God requires an open mind, an attentive heart, and a soul thirsty for meaning, God's meaning in God's Word.

Spiritual proclamation of the Word requires a thoughtful pondering of the meaning of the words in the text and reflection on how these words are to be proclaimed so that they might exercise their power. This process demands oral interpretation skills: attention to the structure of the text, its punctuation and its overall intention; emphasis on verbs and nouns, and never the prepositions; an open diaphragm, full lungs, and projection. But the process is deeper still. In prayerful preparation, the proclaimer of the Word must allow the text to resound in mind and heart for its meaning: meaning for the writer of the text, the words on the page, the listeners, and for the one proclaiming. Not the words of the text of the Scriptures and the Eucharistic Prayer, and not the books, but the meaning of the text heard in the proclaiming is the Word of God for us. That meaning—intentionally, carefully, prayerfully, and reverently proclaimed—changes the life of the proclaimer over time, and the lives of the listeners as well.

---

[10] Genesis 1:3, 9, 14-15, 20-21, 24, 26-27, 28-30.

[11] John 1:1-5, 14.

[12] Hebrews 4:12.

Superficial "looking over" the text of the Scriptures, then "reading them out loud" before the assembly, may get words heard, but it will never bring the Word to life. Rote rattling through the Eucharistic Prayer as if it is incidental—and the paucity in the number of Eucharistic Prayers leaves priests extremely familiar with them—will get Mass said but will inspire no one. Each proclamation of the Scriptures must be approached as if the word is fresh, new, and powerfully alive. The same is true for each proclamation of the Eucharistic Prayer.

When the Word is proclaimed in such a way that the minister personally recedes and becomes, because of his or her prayer, a conduit for God, then the proclaimer and the listeners are touched by the creative and life-giving power of the Word. When the Eucharistic Prayer is proclaimed as if the church ceiling has been sundered and the white hot sun of God's presence is visible and approaching, then priest and people are forever changed in its praying. When the proclamation of the Word is prayerfully prepared and prayerfully done well, then God is alive and active, and the world is recreated in the proclamation of the Word.

### v. The Liturgy of the Hours

Yet another element of tending the Word is the daily praying of the Liturgy of the Hours. The *breviary* or *divine office,* as priests often call it, is a many-times-per-day steeping in the word that all ordained ministers promise at the time of diaconate ordination.

The Liturgy of the Hours is offered to the Church as a way of structuring time for prayer throughout the day. It consists of resources for seven prayer events. One, the Office of Readings, is for prayer during the night. It is a set of three psalms and two readings, one from Scripture and one a reflection from an ancient and venerable theologian or teacher in the tradition. Two offices, Morning Prayer for sunrise and Evening Prayer for sunset, are viewed as the major hinges of the day. They comprise two psalms and a canticle, a reading, a response, a set gospel canticle for each office and intercessions, ending with the Lord's Prayer. Three more structured events for prayer at mid-morning, mid-day and mid-afternoon, often called the *little offices,* consist of three short psalms and a brief reading and response. The final office of the day, Night Prayer, is set for before bed. It consists of one psalm, a reading and a response, and a song to the Blessed Virgin Mary.

The overarching structure for the seven offices each day follows a four-week cycle, which in turn is set within the five liturgical seasons. The Liturgy of the Hours is also framed for the liturgical celebration of particular occasions as well as each and every single day throughout the entire liturgical year. Called "the prayer of the Church" in the tradition, the Liturgy of the Hours offers the whole Church the absolute assurance that, at any given moment of the day, the Church is greeting the rising sun, opening to the final coming of the Lord, and praising God at every moment in-between. The Liturgy of the Hours holds the Church profoundly within time even as it leads the Church to a radical transcendence of time in the celebration of time throughout the day.

The Liturgy of the Hours is profoundly connected to the identity and integrity of the ordained because they publicly promise to pray it. The purpose of that promise, and the Liturgy of the Hours itself, is to call them—and every Christian as the *General Instruction of the Liturgy of the Hours* would have it[13]—to pray always. That is what a priest's leadership role of tending the Word demands of the priest: praying always.[14]

All liturgy in the Roman Catholic Church is structured as Word, then response. In baptism the Church proclaims the Word, then responds with the water bath. In the Eucharist the Church proclaims the Word, then responds with breaking bread and sharing the cup. In Penance the Church proclaims the Word, then lays on hands. The whole of the Liturgy of the Hours is Word. The Church's response is the living out of the day. The Liturgy of the Hours, and the priest's promise to pray it, calls priests to make the whole of their day a response to the Word, an act of worship.

At an absolute minimum, the Liturgy of the Hours, and the promise to pray it, confront priests with three poignant truths. First, they set for priests and the Church a minimum standard for daily prayer—excluding Mass, about one and one-half hours per day. Second, the structure of the Liturgy of the Hours teaches priests and the Church that human beings cannot go much longer than about three hours without losing focus on God and becoming self-absorbed. Third, the Liturgy of the Hours suggests that true prayer demands a rhythm of both more extended times for prayer during each day and brief times for stopping out of the day and hurling prayer, like a javelin, toward the heavens.

When priests promise to pray the Liturgy of the Hours, they promise to strive to pray always. Their integrity and identity as leaders in the community rest, in part, on their constancy in the striving.

---

[13] "General Instruction of the Liturgy of the Hours," in *The Liturgy of the Hours According to the Roman Rite,* vol. I (New York: Catholic Book Publishers, 1975) 21–98.

[14] 1 Thessalonians 5:17.

### vi. A Word About Teaching

Teaching for the priest finds its meaning in the context of preaching and flows from it. The fundamental purpose of teaching is to touch the souls of the hearers through study, reflection, and discussion. This touching of another's soul is aimed at sharing with the disciple and fellow pilgrim how one might look at the world and interpret it in faith, how one might look at one's own life and choose within it the way of life Christ has taught us. Teaching for the priest necessarily includes formation in the content of the Scriptures and the tradition, the wide considerations necessary for living the moral life, the practice of sharing faith, and the principles of participatory leadership. The priest as teacher ideally needs to afford the student maximum opportunity to openly discuss and freely reflect on his or her own experience, thereby seeking to integrate teaching's content with the whole of one's life. Teaching flows from preaching as a ministry of the Word.

### C. BEING FIRST AMONG THE SEARCHERS FOR GOD

Priestly presidency within the eucharistic assembly implicitly proclaims that the priest is committed to being the first among the searchers for God. That is to say, a priest's leadership ministry calls him to live his days in what Donald Cozzens calls a "contemplative spirit,"[15] what Josef Pieper more traditionally calls *leisure*.[16]

Because of their preaching and presidential ministry, priests must be the people in the midst of contemporary society who take the time to nurture in their lives awe and wonder—in the glory of the sunrise and in the courage of the family who has just lost a teenage daughter. They are called to be open to all human experience: birth, sin, grace, suffering, and death. They are called to a silent and serene pondering on the meaning of human experience: their own, others' and the human experience reflected in great literature and art. They are called to a contemplative laying of this experience before God in order to weave it together with the tradition, interpret it in light of the Gospel, and then move outward with insight to proclaim its meaning and celebrate it in worship.

---

[15] Donald Cozzens, *Sacred Silence: Denial and the Crisis in the Church* (Collegeville: The Liturgical Press, 2002) 159.

[16] Josef Pieper, *Leisure: The Basis of Culture* (New York: Random House, Inc., 1963) especially 41–44.

Living in a contemplative spirit, being people of leisure, means that priests need to take time to pray, study, and be with friends, time to delight in the beauty of creation, the goodness of the human heart, and the eternal truths revealed in the arts and sciences. Their being people of leisure means they need to limit their workweek to about forty-five hours, tops—a dramatic reduction for many priests. Living in a contemplative spirit means that priests have to set priorities for their day, trim their activity, and help the Christian faithful adjust their expectations accordingly. As the life of the patron for priests, St. John Vianney, amply illustrates, constant, grinding work leads only to eating on one's feet, brief and restless sleep, puddles of one's own tears, and an untimely death. Our age demands something different from priests.

In a world bereft of meaning, priests are called to spend their days seeking, proclaiming, and living meaning. In a world exhausted from business, they are called to be for others a place of rest. In a world glutted by booming noise and endless chatter, they are called to be for others a place of tranquility and peace. Josef Pieper writes, "The power to achieve leisure is one of the fundamental powers of the human soul."[17] The ministry of the priest calls him to be a person of leisure, a person of contemplative spirit, if he is to fulfill his leadership role, corporately and individually, as a physician of souls.

**D. INTERCESSORS**

Intercessory prayer is also at the core of a priest's being tender of the Word. The effectiveness of a priest's tending the Word depends on his weaving together, in the midst of the assembly, the Word, current events, and the assembly's deepest needs and desires. The priest's leadership ministry, then, calls him to hold up in prayer daily the groaning of the world and the joys and aches of the people with and among whom he serves. It calls priests to place before God the needs of the pope and bishops, the people of the parish, and the poor and suffering across the city, the state, the nation, and the world. A priest's communion with himself, those he serves, the Church throughout the world, and with the world itself is heightened, deepened, and broadened by his interceding on behalf of the people he serves, the Church, and the world. The text for this intercessory prayer is his own life, his relationships, his community of faith, and the newspaper. Intercessory prayer is integral to the priest's

---

[17] Ibid., 44.

day and to his effective ministry for the sake of and on behalf of the people he serves.

### E. CONCLUSION

Tending the Word sets the standard for a priest's assessment of his personal spiritual health and likely ministerial effectiveness. While superiors, colleagues, or parishioners cannot readily know all the minute particulars described above, they can generally intuit a priest's health through the effectiveness of his ministry of the Word. Nonchalance about his own or the Church's integrity, extensive insight-free preaching, a pattern of fleeting and scattered prayer, endless business or lethargy or crabbiness, ill-considered teaching, hardness to people's needs—these attitudes and states are signals that the priest may be in trouble, that his commitment may be likely breaking down, and that perhaps he is beginning to disintegrate. How could Father Shanley's preaching possibly have been insightful? How could Father Goeghan possibly have offered his parishioners evidence of his prayer? Would their lives, and those of many in the church in the United States, be different today if their bishops, colleagues, or parishioners had been sensitive to what it means for the priest to be a tender of the Word?

In sum, the priest's role as presider over the eucharistic oath-taking calls him to be tender of the community's integrity, tender of the Word, first among the searchers for God, and intercessor for the Church and the world. In other words, he needs to be a leader in holiness by living with personal integrity what presidency in the midst of the eucharistic assembly proclaims him to be. All those around a priest—family, friends, superiors, colleagues, and those with and among whom he serves—need to help a priest be alert, in an ongoing way, to his commitment to spiritual health, or his evident lack of it.

# 12. Being Leaders in Love

## A. LOVE, THEN, CONSISTS IN THIS

Jesus commands us to love one another. We Christians all know and accept the centrality of the command, and the Christian tradition calls it "the great commandment." Preaching and teaching across the ages has called human beings to love of God and neighbor. But the indispensable key to understanding what love is can be found in the First Letter of John.

> In this is love, not that we have loved God but that [God] has loved us and sent his son to be the atoning sacrifice for our sins. Beloved, since God loved us so much, we also ought to love one another.[1]

God's loving us is the source from which all love flows: our love of God and our love of one another. The central experience of the Christian life that sets alight and fires our faithfulness is the experience of God's love. That was true for Jesus. It is true for us.

The baptism of Jesus inaugurates his ministry. In the Synoptic Gospels the pulsating heart of this profound religious experience for Jesus is his deep awareness of being loved.[2] During the baptism for Matthew and Mark, and while at prayer after it in Luke, the skies open, which in Hebrew cosmology places the universe on the edge of annihilation; the Spirit hovers, as he hovered over the primordial dark waters in Genesis 1:1; the Spirit hovers as a dove, like the lone sentinel who brings Noah news of the earth's recreation;[3] and then Jesus hears a thundering voice: "I love you! You are mine! I am with you!" This personal experience of being loved by God so overwhelms Jesus that he flees to the desert for forty days to sort it out, and there he is transformed from Nazareth carpenter to preacher, teacher, healer, and prophet.

---

[1] 1 John 4:10-11.

[2] See Matthew 3:13-17; Mark 1:7-11; and Luke 3:15-22.

[3] Genesis 8:8-12.

When Jesus' face is set toward his passion and death in Jerusalem, the Synoptic Gospels record another, similar experience: the Transfiguration.[4] The cloud that signals the very presence of God, that appeared on Mount Sinai, that led Israel through the desert in Exodus, and that settled in Solomon's Temple at its dedication,[5] envelopes Jesus and his disciples. Moses and Elijah appear. Then a thundering voice is heard: "I love him! He is mine! Listen to him!" This experience of God's love strengthens Jesus and the disciples for the passion and crucifixion to come.

Both of these pivotal experiences of God's love, which set alight and fire Jesus' preaching, teaching, and healing ministry on one hand, and Jesus' ultimate ministry of his passion, death, and resurrection on the other, point to a telling and often neglected truth: the origin of our loving as Jesus would have us love is our knowing, believing, and *experiencing deep within* God's love of us. Thus the aim of all Christian ministry is to inspire and evoke in others, and share with others, the experience of being infinitely loved by God. From this conviction and experience, our love for God and our love for one another flows.

Author Brennan Manning calls this experience of God's love "the wisdom of tenderness."[6] He offers these observations:

> The wisdom of tenderness allow us to love our whole life story and know that we have been graced and made beautiful by the providence of our past history. "Even from my sins," wrote Augustine of Hippo, "God has drawn good." All the wrong turns in the past, the detours, the mistakes, the moral lapses—*everything* that's irrevocably ugly or painful melts and dissolves in the light of accepted tenderness.[7]

The wisdom of tenderness is available to all Christians, indeed to all human beings, as God's free gift. But among human beings, the priest as presider and preacher in the eucharistic assembly needs to have had this experience. He needs to understand it, live within it and do the spiritual work to set the stage for inspiring and evoking it in others. This experience of and conviction about God's tender love for us grounds all our loving, whether of God or of others, and it is the engine that fires a sin-

---

[4] See Matthew 17:1-9; Mark 9:2-10; Luke 9:28-36; and 2 Peter 1:16-19.

[5] 1 Kings 8:10-13.

[6] Brennan Manning, *The Wisdom of Tenderness: What Happens When God's Fierce Mercy Transforms Our Lives* (San Francisco: Harper/SanFrancisco, 2002). See 21–54.

[7] Ibid., 32–33.

cere and committed Christian way of life. The priest needs to be a leader in love.

## B. THE LIFTING OF SHAME

If we ponder what Jesus says about forgiveness,[8] we come to see that we are obliged as Christians to do all we can to help everyone understand that they have dignity and value, that they deserve respect and reverence, that the Father loves them just as much as the Father loves Jesus. We need to do everything in our power, in other words, to lift shame from others. This obligation also means that we must open to God and others for our own shame to be lifted.

Shame is the opposite of healthy self-love. It is a sense of personal worthlessness, an inner alienation that leaves a person feeling negated, valueless, without dignity. The most profound image of shame in literature is the prodigal son in the pigsty. He is alienated from his father and family as squanderer of his inheritance, from his God and religious tradition as he feeds pigs, from his body and himself as he stands, starving, ankle-deep in mud. The words of his shame are these: "Father, I no longer deserve to be called your son."[9] With these words he proclaims his alienation from the core of his identity and dignity, the one thing that can never change: that he is his father's son. When he returns, it is at precisely these words that the father breaks in and calls for the robe, ring, shoes, and party. Because shaming another person is the essence of hate, the father pleads with his older son, too, to lift his brother's shame—to acknowledge his brother's worth, honor his value, respect and reverence his human dignity, and extend him the tender love that he himself knows. Jesus calls all who would follow him to do the same for everyone.

## C. HUMAN SEXUALITY

The role of the priest demands that he be a leader in love. An area of human life that is most sensitive in this regard is sexuality, a person's placing himself or herself in the world as lover and available for being loved. Consequently, I would examine a priest's leadership in love relative to four elements of sexual wholeness: healthy sexual self-awareness,

---

[8] Luke 15:11-35 (parable of the Prodigal Son); Matthew 18:23-35 (parable of the Unforgiving Debtor); Luke 7:36-50 (story of the woman washing Jesus' feet in the house of Simon the Pharisee); John 7:3-11 (story of the woman caught in adultery).

[9] Luke 15:19, 21b.

healthy sexual attitudes, healthy relationships in general, and healthy relationships among priests.

### i. Healthy Sexual Self-awareness

Human sexuality is "the most powerful force on the planet,"[10] Ronald Rolheiser writes in *The Holy Longing*. He goes on . . .

> We wake up in the world and in every cell of our being we ache, consciously and unconsciously, sensing that we are incomplete, unwhole, lonely, cut-off, a little piece of something that was once part of a whole.[11]

In the face of this profound reality integral to every human person, priests have promised celibate chastity, to be radical witnesses that God's love is enough for them, that God's love—in the midst of the community of faith—can relieve the ache, make human beings whole, transform loneliness into solitude, and bring human beings to the fullness of life. Yet desire continues to burn within priests because they are human beings. Consequently, priests need to nurture in their lives a healthy self-awareness as sexual beings.

Experts tell us that many people tend to under-process their sexual inclinations and keep some sexual experiences closeted because they feel shame. Sexual health calls all human beings, priests among them, to grow in awareness of sexual attractions and desires, to name them and to talk about them with people they trust. A priest's forthrightly facing his sexuality and sexual experience, examining his fantasies and inclinations, being ruthlessly honest about his sexual compulsions (if any), and exploring as best he can his sexual motivations offers him the opportunity to clarify who he is sexually and sort through how he ought to think and act sexually. This probing, naming, and talking about it increases any human being's chances of getting the support and establishing the accountability he or she needs to maintain sexual health. The same is true for the priest. Sex shrouded in darkness leaves anyone at risk of acting out of passions that can cause others and one's self great pain and harm.

Human sexuality is immensely complex, a mystery. Most people have intense feelings about sex, some people feel hurt and shame around it, and virtually all experience surprises and make mistakes. All human beings, therefore, including priests, need to continually monitor their sex-

---

[10] Ronald Rolheiser, O.M.I., *The Holy Longing: The Search for a Christian Spirituality* (New York: Doubleday, 1999) 193. See 192–212 for his full treatment of a spirituality of sexuality.

[11] Ibid., 194.

ual self-awareness to stay healthy. Priests, like the rest of humankind, need to keep probing, naming, and talking about their sexuality if they are to grow in healthy sexual self-awareness.

## ii. Healthy Sexual Attitudes

Priests also need to nurture in their lives healthy sexual attitudes. The sexual fire that burns within is a given for all people; sexual drive is a gift from God. In Rolheiser's words,

> It is the drive for love, communion, community, friendship, family, affection, wholeness, consummation, creativity, self-perpetuation, immortality, joy, delight, humor and self-transcendence.[12]

Their sexual desires and attractions leave many celibates with enormous sexual tension, what Rolheiser calls the pains of "sexual inconsummation."[13] This tension is a kind of poverty. Priests pledge to live in it all their lives. But they must attend to their sexual tension vigilantly if they are to live celibacy faithfully.

Informed by sexual self-awareness, a priest's sexual tension calls him—just like all single and married people across the world—to reflect carefully on his sexual boundaries. Priests, like all human beings, have important decisions to make about who touches them and whom they touch, about expressions of affection public and private, about whom they can and cannot be with and in what contexts. They have important decisions to make about how they deal with what stimulates them sexually: situations, clothing, TV programs, advertisements, internet and print pornography, the beach, the shower, bed. They also have important decisions to make about their diet, sleep, exercise, the amount and intensity of their work, and their consumption of alcohol. All of these concerns factor into healthy sexuality. What matters most in all these considerations—as for anyone who would be sexually healthy, whatever his or her state in life—is that the priest be coldly realistic about himself, respectfully reverent toward others, ever-mindful that he is changing all the time, and that he remains faithful to his commitments, for him celibacy. Like everyone else on the planet, priests have made and will make mistakes.

The mystery and power of sex, and its link to covenant commitment, call priests to understand that there is no way to be celibate and, at the

---

[12] Ibid.

[13] Ibid., 204. See his full treatment, 204–12.

same time, have a relationship tending toward genital sexual expression. Celibate commitment and sexual acting out are contradictory. As the Church has learned so painfully in recent years, attempting to hold this contradiction together will sooner or later disembowel a priest's ministry and hurt deeply, on a scale small and large, others, priests themselves, and the Church.

The sexual tension, pain, and poverty priests experience as celibates call them to reach toward health both inwardly and outwardly.

Celibacy calls the priest to reach toward inward health by learning the facts about human sexuality, growing in sexual self-awareness, and striving to become ever more comfortable talking about sexuality. It means laying before God, even when the fires burn hot, his longing and sense of incompleteness, his grandiose imaginings, and his fantasies. God can hear any and all of what human beings have to unload. Before God all of us can very often sort it out and let it go.

Celibacy calls priests to reach toward outward health by sharing a life of compassion, affection, work, and play, with the full range of those with whom they share life and faith, respecting and accepting both genders. It calls them to open up generously so they can share attentively with others their joys and hopes, their fears and their sorrows, and so the priest can invite them to share his, too.

Celibacy calls a priest as well to life-giving creativity and generativity in all that he is, says, and does. That is to say, priests need a life! They deserve time for self-expression and self-development—from playing the piano and creative writing to gardening and building things, from hunting, fishing, and breeding dogs to the theater, travel, and researching family genealogy. The more creative and generative priests are, as is true for all people, the healthier their attitudes toward all of life, including sexuality.

Healthy sexual attitudes require a lifetime's striving.

### iii. Healthy Relationships in General

All human beings need healthy relationships of intimate trust, congenial companionship, and just plain affection and fun. We need them with men and women, married and single, young, old, and peers.

Living within healthy relationships means that priests, like everyone else, need in their lives people who can hear whatever they have to say, accept them as they are, help them stay honest, and hold them accountable. Having healthy relationships means that a priest has several people in his life with whom he can be straightforwardly open, confident that they will offer helpful perspective, keep his secrets, and occasionally call him to task. Healthy relationships are mutually hospitable. They bring to life mutual freedom, honesty, accountability, laughter, and peace.

One measuring stick a celibate living alone might use to assess his relative health in relationships might be this: am I communicating every day with at least one intimate friend? Another might be: when I am sad or angry or sexually aflame, do I eat, drink, or stay busy, or do I call a trusted friend? Yet another might be: am I available to my friends when they call on me?

### iv. Healthy Relationships among Priests

Priests also need to have healthy relationships among themselves, particularly from the perspective of their being a community comprised of both homosexually and heterosexually oriented men. The sexual misconduct scandal raised to the fore the question of ordaining homosexual men. Beginning in October 2002, it was reported that a document was circulating in Vatican circles that would exclude homosexual men from being ordained. The question of homosexuality and ordination is an important modern concern for the Church.[14]

In fact, thousands of priests in the United States are homosexually oriented. In a presbytery of three hundred priests, for instance, the statistics suggest that some sixty to perhaps one hundred thirty or more are homosexually oriented. As a whole Church we must in justice and charity face this fact. And though the posture is counter-cultural, we also as a Church need to begin to reconcile ourselves to the likelihood that, whatever bishops might think or a Vatican congregation might promulgate, homosexually oriented men, as they have always been, will continue to be among our priests. What follows is offered to provoke creative thinking and perhaps help bring us in the U.S. church to some calm about what simply is.

But first, it would be well to restate some important distinctions.

The homosexual man, like the heterosexual man, is oriented toward peers. Sexual orientation toward children, *pedophilia*, is a completely separate matter, and, clinically, a compulsion. Acting on it is also criminal.[15] Attraction to teen-agers, *ephebophilia*, is also a separate matter. It

---

[14] "Homosexuality, Priesthood Don't Mix, Officials Say," *The Catholic Spirit* (vol. 7, no. 37, October 17, 2002) 10. Also see "Vatican Prepares Draft Against Admitting Gays to Ordination," in "Signs of the Times," *America* (vol. 187, no. 12, October 21, 2002) 4.

[15] See Donald Cozzens, "Time to Face the Facts," *The Tablet* (May 4, 2002) 8–9.

suggests sexual underdevelopment. Though acting on it is criminal, experts attest that it says little, in itself, about a person's orientation.[16] The homosexually oriented man is different from these. He is essentially oriented toward peers. This point is presumed in what follows.

It is also presumed that the homosexually oriented man and the heterosexually oriented man are more alike than they are different. The clerical culture has all sorts of assumptions about the homosexual man's innate artistic sensitivity, his love of liturgy, his preference for being with others like himself, his developed "feminine side," and so on. While these assumptions might bear scrutiny for some, they are essentially stereotypes. I think the talk about the homosexual priest's love of flowing garments particularly ironic given the history of clerical dress and vesture, not to mention that the higher a cleric rises, the more elaborate the garments and the more attention given to them.[17]

As a society we are prone to still more assumptions. Predominant is the notion that if a person admits he is homosexual that means he is sexually active. Another is the broadly felt male anxiety that every man is somehow at risk in the presence of any homosexual man, as if the inscrutable mystery of on-and-off sexual attraction did not apply to homosexually oriented people. Among priests these attitudes often seem rooted in a kind of nervous defensiveness about their all-male clerical culture and, as Cozzens puts it in *Sacred Silence,* "the deeply held belief that gay priests and religious are somehow damaged goods."[18] These attitudes, however, are all a form of prejudice.

Experts tell us that sexual identity is not a tidy package but a highly complex reality. It likely falls on a continuum and is contingent on many factors. The categories *homosexual* and *heterosexual* are very much too tidy. Beyond the complexity, though, wherever a person might find him or her self on the continuum between being purely homosexual or purely

---

[16] See ch. 2 above, and Melvin Blanchette and Gerald D. Coleman, "Priest Pedophiles," *America* (vol. 186, no. 13) 18–21. Also see Joseh J. Guido, "The Importance of Perspective: Understanding the Sexual Abuse of Children by Priests," *America* (vol. 186, no. 11) 21–23. For a simple and popular distinguishing among these see William Bausch, *Breaking Trust: A Priest Looks at the Scandal of Sexual Abuse* (Mystic, Conn.: Twenty-Third Publications, 2002) 39–43.

[17] James Martin, s.j., "The Church and the Homosexual Priest," *America* (vol. 183, no. 14), offers a complementary perspective on the differences homosexuality makes for a priest. He also suggests the areas of creativity and spirituality might be distinctive contributions from homosexually oriented priests. I think those suggestions interesting, but arguable.

[18] Donald Cozzens, *Sacred Silence: Denial and the Crisis in the Church* (Collegeville: The Liturgical Press, 2002) 129.

heterosexual, all humans are far greater than their sexual orientation. They are all far more like each other than different.[19]

Looking beyond terminological confusion and stereotypes,[20] we find that homosexually oriented priests likely do bring to ministry some differences.

First, most homosexually oriented priests have probably experienced what sociologists call *liminality* to a greater extent than the heterosexually oriented. They have known what it is to feel compelled to keep their sexual identity secret for fear of rejection and what it is to confide their orientation to another only to be rejected and become an object of gossip. They know the public judgment that what they experience as an inclination emerging from deep within as they grew up, the institutional Church regards as "intrinsically disordered."[21] They know what it is to be publicly patronized by a Church that rejects their natural inclination, labels "immoral" their acting on it, and is reportedly considering banning them from ordained ministry while it says, at the same time, it accepts them. Many of the homosexuals among priests have known intense self-doubt and shame. This typically years-long experience of liminality leaves many of them with a deep understanding of sexual tension, sexual self-discipline, and the pain of inconsummation. The homosexually oriented man often comes to ordination with profound insight into human experiences like exodus, exile, alienation, shame, poverty, hunger for wholeness, and eschatological hope. This understanding is a terribly hard won gift for ministry.

Second, the homosexually oriented among priests typically bring an unusual ease and comfort in relating with most men. Beyond the ordinary

---

[19] See George A. Aschenbrenner, s.j., *Quickening the Fire in Our Midst: The Challenge of Diocesan Priestly Spirituality* (Chicago: Loyola Press, 2002) 122–23, where he writes, "The real issue concerns honesty and respect. Personal (not public) honesty about sexual orientation (whether homosexual or heterosexual) is needed, as is respect for each other as united in priestly service, taking care not to get trapped in the exclusive enclave of a subculture . . . . a man's sexual orientation is not the most important issue about him in seminary formation."

[20] See Donald Cozzens, *The Changing Face of the Priesthood* (Collegeville: The Liturgical Press, 2000) 100, 135.

[21] See Andrew R. Baker, "Ordination and Same Sex Attraction," *America* (vol. 187, no. 9, September 30, 2002) 7–9, that also refers to same sex attraction as "aberrant," unable to image God, never able to contribute to the good of society, "tending toward a corrupt end," among other things. Baker's article receives response in later issues. Edward Vacek, "'Acting More Humanely': Accepting Gays Into the Priesthood," *America* (vol. 187, no. 20, December 16, 2002) 10–14, offers a detailed critique of Baker's "trial balloon." In the same issue, also see Jon Guller, "On 'Straightening Out' Catholic Seminaries," 7–9.

talk of sports, tools, politics and jobs, many American males are ill at ease probing the deeper currents of human life. Because many homosexually oriented men have a highly attuned, intuitive interest in other men, they often have a facility in achieving with men mutual intimacy and personal self-revelation. Some homosexual priests may tend to seek out other homosexuals. Very many feel no need and are at ease sharing faith and inviting to deeper personal insight men of all ages and ways of life. This interest in attentive mentoring of, and friendship with, males is also a gift for ministry.

Third, homosexually oriented priests often bring to ministry an unusual ease and comfort in relating with women. Many American females feel left out—of the church especially. They have known stereotype, patronizing, exclusion, and having to be something they would rather not be in order to succeed. Because homosexually oriented males have known similar experiences, they often understand and empathize with women in ways other men cannot. Moreover, the homosexually oriented priest's lack of sexual interest in women eliminates the sexual static women typically anticipate in relationship with a male. The silencing of this static often frees a homosexual man for deep, close, and utterly nonthreatening relationships with women. This, too, is a gift for ministry.

In spite of the hand wringing, the homosexually oriented man often brings to ordained ministry not a lack but a fullness different from but equal to what many heterosexually oriented men bring. There is and will be no crisis among priests regarding the sexual identity question so long as the ordained remain attentive and faithful to their personal and spiritual integrity, sexual health, celibate commitment, and the ordinary expectations our society has about normal, courteous, respectful human behavior.[22]

That is to say, whether someone is homosexually or heterosexually oriented, similar standards need to apply. Sexual promiscuity and sexual compulsions are negative indicators for ordination. Sexual ambivalence or seeming to be sexually "out-of-touch" suggest lack of self-knowledge and are also negative indicators. An aggressive attitude about one's sexual orientation, or a need to publicly talk about it, suggest a lack of self-acceptance and are negative indicators. An inclination toward swishy camp is as negative an indicator for ordination as an inclination toward macho bravado, or having no affect at all. In word, aspect, and demeanor, all priests need to blend comfortably and with relatively little

---

[22] See Cozzens, *The Changing Face of the Priesthood,* 97–110.

splash into the wide array of males and females of all ages and walks of life that they serve in their ministry settings. Priests all have to be willing and able to commit to faithful celibacy.

One important factor that has led to the sexual misconduct scandal and other forms of sexual acting out among priests is systematic sexual repression. It is counter-productive, therefore, for us in the Church not to provide a safe environment where celibates can talk together about their sexuality concerns, find informed and discerning support toward celibate chastity, and share together their experience of healthy models of both homosexual and heterosexual celibacy.

Continued repression among priests cuts at the core of the Church and priestly ministry. Banning homosexual men from ordained ministry, for instance, were the Vatican to do that, would raise conflicts of integrity among ordained and lay people across Western society. It would undermine Vatican authority as seminaries and bishops unevenly obey. It would be repressive and shaming, while accomplishing, in fact, very little of its aim. As Cozzens writes, "A culture that fosters closeted homosexuality—a 'don't ask, don't tell' culture—is by definition unhealthy. It impedes the spiritual journey of the priest . . . and violates the integrity of his soul."[23] Repression only nurses shame and secrecy among priests, and it prolongs the Church's and priests' problems. It also stunts and even tramples the possibility of tender love.

And so . . . if a very large minority among priests is homosexually oriented, perhaps it is time to consider that fact in the light of faith. Perhaps the presence of homosexual men among our priests is a gift God calls the Church to accept rather than a cause for hand wringing. Perhaps it is time seminaries and dioceses started to shape continuing formation programs to address the needs of the homosexually oriented among the priests and the need for all priests to come together in mutual understanding rather than nervously pretend that the homosexual men aren't there. Perhaps it is time for bishops and priests to accept priests as they are. If priests open their lives to being healthy and normal human beings, the larger Church gives strong evidence that it is more than happy to accept priests as they are.

---

[23] Cozzens, *Sacred Silence*, 130.

## D. CONCLUSION

The promise of celibacy puts sexuality front and center for priests. It is not only a private issue for them but a public one. Because this is so, people pay attention to what they see of a priest's sexual self-awareness and attitudes. They look to priests to model sexual health and healthy personal relationships—with men, women, children, and each other. Sexuality is one of the great common links that priests have with those they serve.

The priest's call to inspire, evoke, and extend the experience of God's tender love for all people, based on the priest's own experience and understanding of it, demands that the priest lead in tenderness, that he model sexual health, that he lead in valuing, respecting, and reverencing the dignity of all human beings. The priest above all should know and nurture, in himself and others, God's promise offered to us all: "I love you! You are mine! I am with you!"

# 13. Being Leaders in Justice

A priest's role calls him to be a leader in justice. Many priests complain that they dislike administration, that it takes them away from real ministry. I would suggest that not only is administration ministry, it is justice ministry. Our tradition defines the virtue of justice as working to establish right order in relationships so as to build up the common good for the sake of the Kingdom. Administration is all about ordering relationships for building up the common good. It is all about justice. It is critical to the life of the Church. It is a ministry entrusted to priests, particularly those entrusted with the care of a particular faith community.

If priests are to be leaders in justice, they need especially to ponder five areas of administration: tending the mission, the Spirit's gifts, the light, their own celibate commitment, and their own way of life.

## A. TENDERS OF THE MISSION

One of the hazards of being a priest is losing sight of the Church's mission and becoming self-absorbed. This pattern is the striking element underneath priests sexually exploiting the young and bishops moving them from parish to parish.

Their leadership role calls priests to take great care to remain clear, always clear, about the mission of the Church. It calls them to remember that the Church's mission is to be a contrast community exemplary in virtue, imitating Jesus Christ in all we say and do, never merely a self-serving corporation. The Church's mission is not to preserve itself but to transform the world. Its mission is to attend to the Lord inwardly, as well as move out into the world preaching, teaching, serving others, and embodying Jesus Christ in word and action. No matter what our local mission statements may say, the first mission of the diocese, the parish, and all ministerial settings is to serve the Church's universal mission to transform the world through and with Jesus Christ in the Holy Spirit.

A priest's leadership role calls him to remain clear as well, always clear, about who is responsible for carrying out the mission. The ordained have a critically important role to fulfill as ministers of communion, holiness, universality, and continuity. They are tenders of the mission. Nonetheless, the mission belongs to all, lay and ordained, because all are Church. Baptism commissions the whole Christian assembly to mission; holy orders intensifies that baptismal commission into leadership. Responsibility for the mission, then, is a common responsibility, not the mission of the ordained alone. A priest's leadership ministry calls him to do everything in his power to help all he serves share common responsibility for the one common mission.

Priests' tending the mission is a marvelous antidote to the tendency toward self-preservation, self-protection, and self-absorption inherent in the enclosed clerical culture. It reminds priests that they are about God's business, not their own.

## B. TENDERS OF THE HOLY SPIRIT'S GIFTS

The priest's ministry of leadership demands, too, that he be tender of the Holy Spirit's gifts. Merely filling slots, taking leadership without a sense of fit, neglecting the expertise of those he serves and denial of all sorts—all of which we saw during the sexual misconduct scandal—tempts priests, but it is irresponsible for them to succumb. Tending the Holy Spirit's gifts means essentially three things.

First, it means that priests, particularly leaders of faith communities, need to explicitly place all community decisions under the single question: What does God want of us? The people know when priests are working out their own agendas, manipulating, or evading. The people resent it. When the community a priest serves needs to choose direction, the only question that really matters is, "What does God want of us?" No question is more important or more clarifying for shaping ministry well. The question, "What does God wants of us?" needs to be publicly and firmly placed as the standard of measurement for discernment in all faith community decisions. The priest is responsible for keeping the question in place.

Second, tending the Spirit's gifts means that priests need to invite people broadly to use their God-given gifts. Often beleaguered, priests are tempted to avoid taking the time and spending the energy to invite others to use their gifts. Priests often think it a hassle. It risks the results being less or other than they would wish. It dilutes their control. They are often tempted to either stick with the tried and true or just do it themselves. But helping an ever-broader range of people use their gifts from the Holy Spirit is central to effective servant leadership for the priest. It is also right at the heart of what the tradition means by "ordering the ministries."

Third, tending the Spirit's gifts means that pastors especially need to keep the large view, the vision, in their communities. In our era the Church needs pastors especially to be more like a bishop than a country pastor in how they spend their time, shape their day, and structure their relationships. Many pastors, after all, serve more people, in more complex circumstances, with greater needs, than ever did the great bishop saints Augustine and Basil, or Albert the Great, or even John Carroll.

Leadership in our time calls priests to tend the Holy Spirit's gifts in ways that replace confusion, exclusion, secrecy, and resentment with clarity, inclusiveness, openness, and gracious collaboration.

### C. TENDERS OF THE LIGHT

Again and again during 2002 the church in the United States heard the call for transparency, for letting the light shine in the Church. What does that mean? It demands at least these three practices.

First, transparency demands that priests invite those they serve to participate in shaping the life of the community by helping lead it. Priests, particularly pastors, need to share decision-making. Though some deliberations require confidentiality, though the pastor has to distinguish occasionally between consultative and deliberative decisions, all matters of any importance need to be brought before parishioner leadership groups. Major concerns require that the whole community be invited into the decision-making process. Breadth at the table offers longer history, wider perspective, and deeper insight. It usually keeps everyone more honest, too. Besides, the community life being shaped is common property. The people expect participation. In many instances they are more capable than the priest is. If guidelines are defined and limits are clear, prayerful participation and discerning shared decision-making around each of the parish's ministries and the life of the parish as a whole are worth it, and a great gift. As a pastor I have gotten into trouble only when I have acted on my own, never when we have acted together.

Second, transparency demands forthright communication. What the ministry community is doing and why, and what it means for the community and the larger Church and the world, needs to be communicated over and over again. Communication in our faith communities is never enough, as anyone who has lived in one knows well. It needs to be frequent and multimedia before people grasp it. Priests also need to publicly apologize when they fail. They need, too, to remind people that communication is a two-way street, a back and forth process. Effective, careful, appropriate communication is critical to transparency.

Third, in our age the priest needs to go the extra mile. He needs to audit the books on a regular basis, or at least do a regular financial review, to maintain a strong sense of fiscal responsibility and accountability. Rectory living expenses need to be available in detail to decision-making bodies and in general to everyone. He needs to publicly subject himself to evaluation and review at set intervals. He needs to devise and implement a means to audit community participation and decision-making structures and let the people he serves weigh in on the effectiveness of these structures. Pastors need to have at least yearly open forums for parish-wide discussion of any and all community concerns. These practices are all, if occasionally bumpy, wonderfully well received in the main, and they make a huge difference in a faith community.

Transparency sheds light on all a priest says and does. It also builds trust. Holding cards close to the chest, trying to manipulate outcomes, evasion, and denial all undercut trust and create suspicion because they proclaim that the priest trusts neither those he serves nor the Holy Spirit. If the priest is consistently transparent in the administration of the faith community he serves, the habit of transparency cannot but eventually filter upwards. As tenders of the light, priests must let the light shine on all they say and do.

## D. TENDERS OF THEIR OWN CELIBATE COMMITMENT

For all of the contemporary questions and controversy surrounding celibacy, the priest's commitment to it is deeply connected with the common good of the Church for the sake of building up the Kingdom. Though many in the Church in our time might be put off by the thought, celibacy has a direct impact on the Church's stewardship of its goods and is intended as a stark and pronounced statement that the goods are not at all for ancillary purposes but for its mission. That is to say, celibacy is an act of justice, by the priest and by the Church, for the sake and on behalf of the Church's mission to the world.

It is well known that a major concern of the Church in the Middle Ages was the question of the inheritance of church goods and property. When the priest died, did his residence belong to his wife and children, or to the Church? What goods in the house belonged to the family, and what goods to the Church? What is the Church's obligation to the maintenance of the family's living for the future if, say, a priest died at thirty-two with a wife and four children?

In the face of these realities, the Church's mandating celibacy has the effect of focusing its financial and property assets more closely to the upkeep only of its ministers. The priest's celibate commitment eases the financial burden of any given ecclesial community who would otherwise have to maintain a priest's family. It eases the burden of the Church's or the priest's needing to be preoccupied about questions of family financial support or inheritance.

In our relatively provincial, nuclear family perspective, we in the United States would tend to approach these issues with a simple, "Pay the priest a larger salary, like the Protestants do." We certainly could do that, and already do for the relatively few married priests across the country. Across the globe, however, ecclesial circumstances vary widely. Some priests in India still live in huts and bathe in the village well each morning. Some in Venezuela live in mud and tin shacks. Some in Tanzania must give their lives to roadless travel, meeting their people at a single tree in the midst of an open plain, for instance, because their parish is so widely scattered and desperately poor. I have been with these priests in these places. The Church is present to these communities in some measure because celibacy and personal heroism combine to make gospel proclamation and church life possible. Had these priests a wife and family, the likelihood of their ministry in these places, and thus the life of the Church, would be considerably diminished.

The connection between celibacy and justice ought to have a very practical appeal for Americans especially. For instance, many of us in the United States would be more at ease offering our monetary gifts to a charity in which 98 percent goes to the underserved, and only 2 percent to administration of the program. We are more hesitant, and somewhat suspicious, when the overhead is 30 percent and what gets to the underserved is only 70 percent. Many among us actually research this kind of information before we make gifts. This instinct has to do with our sense of justice, specifically distributive justice. In a significant way, the distribution of goods and burdens that celibacy allows relative to leadership ministry is similar to the charities example. Celibacy allows for a greater investment of our stewardship gifts in ministries and a lesser investment in tangential support.

The perspective offered here is not meant to be a major defense of celibacy. It is simply intended to be declarative. Celibacy is an act of justice both for the priest and for the Church. It is a kind of stewardship, through which the priest offers the gift of himself so as to make it possible for the maximum amount of the people's gifts (the Church's resources) to be directed toward the Church's mission in the world rather than the priest's family. In the context of the Church's universal mission, this stewardship is massive and generous indeed. If a priest has made this stewardship commitment, he is obliged in justice to keep it.

### E. TENDERS OF THEIR OWN WAY OF LIFE

With the connections between celibacy and justice made explicit, and when light-shining administrative practices are firmly in place, other justice questions open up. The following are two concerns about which priests have somewhat less latitude. They are central, however, to clerical culture and a priest's life, and to questions of justice. The areas are priests' living and money.

In the age of the cell phone and palm pilot, abundant apartments and townhouses, economical motels and ready transportation, a priest really has little need for the rectory in order to be available, share community living, or accommodate the missionary. Clerical culture would be transformed hugely if most rectories across the country were renovated for other use, sold, or razed. Imagine the impact on everyone if the priest lived out in the middle of the community he serves. What would the impact be if a parish-owned residence in the neighborhood was valued in accord with local rates and monitored by an independent board and the priest was required to pay those rates and be publicly accountable to that board? How about the priest managing his own housekeeping, laundry, and cooking bills, his own maintenance and household bills, rather than the parish taking care of all that? Everybody else lives this way, why not priests?

The residence questions raise the salary question. Imagine how clerical culture would be transformed if priests were compensated with, say, $45,000 to $55,000 and a typical benefits package, without all the frills so many enjoy in the name of being free for service and living simply? The rest of the staff are compensated this way, why not the priests? Would not the priest better answer the call to pastoral simplicity, far better understand the life situation of those he serves, and far more meaningfully identify with them if he were housed and compensated like they are and if he lived among them and like they do?

These two matters are only to some extent in a priest's control. The deadening effects of custom are no small hurdle in addressing them.

They are also scary because they cut real close. Still, if priests worked toward changes like these, they would go a long way toward transforming many of the more problematic elements of the clerical culture.

## F. CONCLUSION

Administration is justice ministry: working to establish right order in relationships so as to build up the common good for the sake of the Kingdom. It is the ministry of the vast majority of priests. For priests to fail to tend the mission and the Spirit's gifts, communicate thoroughly or let the light shine on what they are doing, to fail to keep their celibacy commitment or work toward change in the most basic structures of their lives is unjust. These failures place the people with and among whom priests serve at a distance from the Gospel and ecclesial life. They undermine the common good, compromise the priest, and even bring those served, at times, to the brink of loss of faith. Priestly injustice is at the nub of the sexual misconduct crisis that brought our national church to its knees, and still threatens.

If priests took the Gospel call seriously and trusted the work of the Holy Spirit, they could offer the world *the model* of just administration that it so desperately needs. They could also offer the Church the model of faith and hope it so desperately needs.

# 14. The Spirit and the Bride Say "Come!"

A king wished to give his daughter in marriage. The princess was widely known to be a woman of radiant beauty, keen intelligence, and abundant gifts of skill and personality. Knowing that many suitors would desire the princess' hand, the king determined to have a series of ordeals through which eligible knights and princes from far and wide might strive for his daughter's hand, and so it was.

When time came for the final ordeal, three princes remained. The ordeal was this. A chest of gold was placed in a tree on the shore of a frozen lake. The princes were led to the shore opposite the tree with the treasure. Then the herald announced: the one who can walk a perfectly straight course across the lake to the tree and treasure will win the hand of the princess and have for his own the chest of gold. Then the contest began.

The first prince glanced across the frozen lake to the tree and treasure, then stepped out onto the ice. As he walked, he carefully watched his feet, placing one in front of the other, one in front of the other, all the way across the icy lake. When he reached the opposite shore, he looked up. He had veered far to the left of the tree and treasure.

The second prince thought, "I am not going to make his mistake." So when the second prince stepped out onto the ice, he placed his feet one in front of the other heel to toe, heal to toe. He carefully watched his feet as he walked across the lake so that the heel of one foot was perfectly aligned with the toe of the other all the way across. When he reached the opposite shore, he looked up. He had veered far to the right of the tree and treasure.

The third prince riveted his eyes to the tree and treasure, stepped out onto the icy lake and began to walk. The prince never, for an instant, took his eyes off the tree and treasure as he walked. When he reached the tree, he turned to look back. He and all around beheld that the prince had walked a perfectly straight course across the lake. So, the prince won the princess' hand and the chest of gold, and they lived happily ever after.

In our age the Church is invited to consider the transformation of its clerical culture. Most of us in the Church, ordained and lay, would accept the notion that a clerical culture that would leave priests set apart, held above others, and basking in clubby privilege is a form of looking at our feet. It also is true that an uncritical and passive acceptance of the clerical culture as it exists today is another form of looking at our feet.

Priests have given up the dinner bell and now cook for themselves. Their prestige has been tarnished. Yet the Church's continuing lack of reflection upon the clerical culture seems a somewhat dense and timid looking at our feet that leads us to stray from the chest of gold, the hand of the princess, and living happily ever after. We need to begin the hard work of bringing about the transformation of the clerical culture.

## A. CULTURAL TRANSFORMATION IS POSSIBLE

Like water for fish, the clerical culture is the medium that has formed and nurtured the ordained in their ministry. The artifacts, patterns of relationship, and universe of ideas that constitute it sustain the ordained; priests take them for granted. The clerical culture is central to priests' lives for good and for ill. And though priests do not preside over the culture, they do perpetuate at least some elements of it every day of their lives. Still, while all of the contradictions in the clerical culture may not be eradicated, they can be lessened.

Though the eleven contradictions are deeply woven into the material, ideational, and relational fabric of priestly life, none of them is integral to ordained ministry. All of them are changeable. Clerical formation can occur closer to the real world of men and women and children, toward which it is ultimately aimed, and the vast middle that is the contemporary Church, rather than be so withdrawn into a semi-monastic, essentially all-male community setting with little relationship to ministry's future. Fuller information about human sexuality, compassionate and open-minded acceptance of people's place on the continuum of sexual orientation, greater candor about personal struggles with sexual continence, open discussion of and practical help with sexual struggles, and deeper reflection about the spiritual grounding that motivates self-discipline toward sexual continence—all of these are possible within celibacy formation.

A respectful balance can be struck between accountability to superiors and to the people with and among whom priests serve. Bishops and priests can be interdependent and cooperative in their relationship rather than paternal and adolescent. Day-to-day professional life can be structured to more congruently and graciously blend gospel ministry and corporate responsibility for the servant leader. Fuller information can be shared about, and a more appropriate balance can be established between, a priest's professional limits and the expectations of the ministry staff and the faithful. Many more contexts can be created for reflection and discussion about how to boundary personal relationships so priests can both lead well and get the support they need and deserve.

Fractures among priests and in the Church as a whole can be forthrightly discussed and even healed with discerning listening and compassionate care. Priests can receive sufficient financial and residential security to allay their fear of the future, diminish their temptation to acquisitiveness, and support them toward living Gospel simplicity. Integrity and uprightness can be nurtured and nourished in the lives of priests, together with honest acceptance of personal frailty.

This kind of change begins with concerted effort on the part of some in the Church who strive for the persistent, gradual building of consensus toward change on the part of all. Such change demands frank discussion of the contradictions and other concerns as well. It necessitates careful planning as well as the restructuring of priestly formation and priestly accountability. Cultural transformation is, foremost, a spiritual work that calls for change in mindset, relationship patterns, and material reality among all who share ecclesial life. The spiritual elements of the transformation can begin in each and all of us immediately. But who is "us"?

## B. THE "WHO" OF TRANSFORMATION

What the church in the United States needs in our time is what the venerable lives of the saints would call "reform of the clergy." This project means a renewal of the spirituality and a reform of the way of life for the ordained. It needs to be led by priests, and strongly supported by the laity, who will hold priests accountable and keep priests focused. Reform of the clergy, resting on the teachings of Vatican II, needs to be aimed at both priests and bishops.[1]

---

[1] I find it alarming that contemporary seminary students are polarized into pro-Vatican II and anti-Vatican II positions, and I am inclined to agree with the rector who believes that

Changing clerical culture cannot be, foremost, the work of the laity.[2] Lay people know far less than they realize about what the clerical culture is and how it works, and no matter how much they write, picket, publicize or withhold money, their influence, unfortunately, will be limited in a closed culture. Nor will changing clerical culture be the work of the bishops, who are deeply entrenched in many of its patterns and have a vested interest in keeping it as it is. After all, they have generally been selected to do just that, and though they experience some pressure from within their dioceses, they are significantly pressured as well by the Vatican from whom they hear a couple of times a week. When one is in the boat bailing, fixing the hole is simply not possible. Though the popes make a difference, for instance John XXIII in calling the council, Paul VI in shaping it, and John Paul II in reshaping world politics and complementing the curia's conserving disposition, the Vatican, for all its outward focus, is an inward preoccupied bureaucracy that strives to make the whole Church be what it, the curia, thinks it should be. It listens to those with whom it sympathizes, or, better, who sympathize with it. Underneath the crustiness of its many layers, Vatican breadth and narrowness both preclude its leading change in the clerical culture.

Boston, however, teaches the Church an important lesson. For all of the pressure from the press, picketing by the people, anger from fellow-bishops and Vatican discussion, when fifty priests finally came together and signed a petition that the Cardinal needed to go, the Cardinal went. It took some time for the priests to press, and their pressing occurred within a very large national and international context, but it was effective. The "point persons" for clerical cultural change are priests. When diocesan priests see that clerical cultural change is in their interest, in the interest of the people, in the interest of the universal Church and the gospel mission, then they will apply their energies, begin to transform their own lives spiritually, drum up sufficient support from the laity, and then place enough pressure on the bishops to bring about wide cultural change.

In the end, laity and priests together will reshape the material reality, articulate the ideas, and build the patterns of relationship that will open the bishops and the Church as a whole to change. Lay people today can help motivate and focus priests by framing their concerns, expressing

---

an anti-Vatican II position is, itself, unorthodox. See Katarina Schuth, *Seminaries, Theologates, and the Future of Church Ministry: An Analysis of Trends and Transitions* (Collegeville: The Liturgical Press, 1999) 210–12.

[2] See Donald Cozzens, *Sacred Silence: Denial and the Crisis in the Church* (Collegeville: The Liturgical Press, 2002) 152–54.

their priorities, offering expertise, and marshalling resources to proceed. Nonetheless, though they will be dependent on lay encouragement and resources, priests—the bridges between the people and the hierarchy in the Church—will need to be in the vanguard of clerical cultural change.

In the morass of the Church's current place in the organizational life cycle, even the beginning of change will take much time. Until the priests are motivated, their focus is clear, and they begin to make concerted effort through groups small and large, for example, diocesan presbyteries and the National Federation of Priest Councils, the Church as a whole is stalled. However, it need not remain stalled.

## C. WE NEED TO BEGIN

By describing the clerical culture and its contradictions, I hope to help the church in the United States face the ugly underbelly of its ecclesial life, begin to ponder the contradictions and then ask: what does contemporary clerical culture say about the identity of Jesus Christ in the world? What do I need to do, what do we need to do, to change ourselves and this culture so we can respond authentically to the gospel call to conversion of life and to the Kingdom? As leaders in holiness, love, and justice, the ordained are, by definition, ministers of cultural transformation. If the ordained grow in their commitment to live their call authentically—being faithfilled and hopeful, holy, loving, and just—then the very attitudes and dispositions that lead to change can begin change. If priests and people can begin to point out to one another concretely how seriously the clerical culture hampers priest leadership and Church ministry when it needs to expand it, then even day-to-day acts can achieve the toehold that will eventually lead to wholesale cultural change.

The ministry of clerical cultural transformation will be difficult. Lay people in the Church see only hints of the culture compared to its full reality. Lay sensitivity to it needs to vastly increase so people across the Church can support change. Because priests benefit from the culture, they need to open their eyes to the price the Church's mission pays as they continue to live the culture's contradictions. The elephants in the room remain elephants. Still, we need to begin.

Walking the way toward transformation will cost. It will demand that we as Church deepen our abiding communion with God and live, with rigorous personal integrity, the eucharistic oath we swear and over which priests preside. It will require priests to relate to one another, the whole Church, the world, and themselves differently. It will require that the laity demand that of them. For all the ordeal of it, I believe that the price of walking the way of transformation can bear fruit beyond imagining in a collaborative communion in which we all as Church, lay and ordained together, grow in love and mission, alive with God.

Through the whole set of circumstances in which the church in the United States finds itself today, the Holy Spirit is inviting us to look up from our feet. The Spirit is calling us to rivet our gaze upon the goal— we the Church: holy, loving, just, faithful, and hope-filled, radiant as a bride adorned for her spouse—and resolutely step forward. In the words of the Scriptures, "the Spirit and the bride say, 'Come!'"[3]

---

[3] Revelation 22:17a.

# Appendix 1. Cleveland Priests' Hopes and Concerns Based on Three Areas of Challenge

## 1. LEADERS IN HOLINESS

*Hopes*

- Recapture the honest balance of spiritual priorities that need to be the foundation of our life and Church. **XX**[1]
- Swearing allegiance to Christ, the Eucharist as oath, should have influence in our heads and our hearts.
- Prayer of the Liturgy of the Hours that leads to the response of daily life is a powerful concept.
- Sacred trust is a beauty of being in the parish; it is a reminder of what we are about.
- Refreshing to hear such a powerful reflection upon the Liturgy of the Hours.
- Service to who we are and what we do (sacramental life) shapes us in who we are and whose we are.
- Call to ministry is from baptism, people are interested in holiness, thirsting for Scripture and homilies.
- The view of leisure as contemplation, our importance of the promise to pray for the Church can be a daily occasion of ordering our day.
- This call encourages us to celebrate with more integrity and call the assembly to be and recognize the presence of Christ.

*Concerns*

- Daily life and its pace prevent us from recognizing and reflecting upon the blessing of life and ministry. Demands on us prevent us from effectively communicating the faith. **XXXXXX**
- We must make our integrity part of our public ministry. Moving from belief to action. We need to develop the preaching of the healing mes-

---

[1] **X** means the item is repeated again.

174

sage of the Word. The challenge to change our expectations and those of the people.

## 2. LEADERS IN LOVE

### *Hopes*

- If we are going to change we must change our own perceptions so as not to fall into a shame-based way of thinking. This is going to be countercultural because our society does not think this way.
- Homosexuals in ministry make a positive contribution. **XXX**
- Openness to talking about sexual issues.
- We are wounded healers, greater self-awareness, and striving to be whole and holy.
- Intimate friendship is essential for healthy sexuality, we must rise above the taboos.
- Our sexuality through greater awareness and spirituality can be a gift to culture and society.
- Healthy relating among priests, the need to get together formally will undo competitiveness and parochialism.
- Choice in rectory living might help but will need motivation.
- Examining the number of work hours.

### *Concerns*

- There is a dearth of professional church and psychological assistance to priests with an understanding of priesthood.
- Writing off homosexuals and repressing the open sharing about sexual and orientation issues.
- Presbyters are still in shame about ourselves.
- Fear of being exposed or found out is often not talked about.
- It makes perfect sense that we should not displace sexuality anxiety with workaholism and alcoholism.
- Lack of self-awareness of sexually suffering priests in our midst.
- The failure of decision makers to take into account the current psychological understanding of sexuality, addiction, accountability, etc.
- Loneliness.

## 3. LEADERS IN JUSTICE

### *Hopes*

- The acknowledgement that something has changed.

- The option to move out of rectories into the neighborhoods. **XXXX**
- That administration and justice go well together is comforting.
- Calling forth and nurturing the gifts of the people is absolutely necessary and needed. **XXXXX**
- Honesty and communicating energize trust and invite others to be responsible for parish life.
- Administration is ministry—think outside the box.
- Light of transparency is something desired by people and modeled by many parishes.

### Concerns

- Sense of exhaustion and frustration with things as they are.
- Possibility of priests mimicking their neighbors may lead to imbalance within the presbyterate.
- Life and ministry cannot take place living on one's own.
- What happens when laity want to buy into clerical culture and when laity fail to fulfill ministerial commitment?
- We cannot do what we have been doing if we are going to start doing all the tasks of homeownership.
- Loss of rectory could damage our accessibility to the parishioners and the way we view our vocation—a job.
- How will we be flexible to assignments if we own our own homes? Efficiency is not our primary value.
- Our living situation is a concern that needs attention.
- The danger of trusteeism when we emphasize the involvement of the laity.
- Just wages for all priests if these changes are made.
- Priests living alone.
- If we do not pull together and make a strategic plan to accomplish our goals, we will not make any progress.

# Appendix 2. Cleveland Priests' Large-Group Discussion Task Force Charges

**SENIOR PRIESTS (THREE) HOPES OR TASKS THAT THE TASK FORCE SHOULD ADDRESS:**

- Priesthood reflecting a balance of holiness, Eucharist, modeling "being."
- Recognition that we are wounded healers needing acceptance of self and others.
- Empowering the people to ministry and fostering the justice that involves a right relationship with God, self, others, and environment.

**RECENTLY ORDAINED (THREE) HOPES OR TASKS THAT THE TASK FORCE SHOULD ADDRESS:**

- More priest gatherings to help us share our stories and the good news of ministry. More convocations (two per year). Sharing in age groups was helpful and make these get-togethers about the joys.
- More trained spiritual directors and make lists available to the priests.
- Rectory living leads to alienation and loneliness, and we need to address it now.
- Empowering people and enabling the gifts of people. Encourage pastoral planning in parishes so that more people get involved thus freeing us to do more priestly things.

**NEW PASTORS (THREE) HOPES OR TASKS THAT THE TASK FORCE SHOULD ADDRESS:**

- Seek a balance of life, prayer, and leisure.
- Greater awareness to promote sexuality as a gift to society and culture.

- Variety of living situations at parishes and other places, staying connected in areas as priests (not just in living situation).

## MID-LIFERS (THREE) HOPES OR TASKS THAT THE TASK FORCE SHOULD ADDRESS:

- Recapturing the honest balance of spiritual priorities that need to be the foundation of life and Church, allegiance to Christ as oath should influence peoples' hearts and minds, people's thirst for spirituality.
- Homosexuals in ministry make a positive contribution; there should be an openness to talking about sexuality. We are all wounded, needing acceptance.
- The option to live out of rectories. **XX**
- The need to nurture the gifts of the people.
- Better communication.

## OTHERS UNDER FORTY-FIVE (THREE) HOPES OR TASKS THAT THE TASK FORCE SHOULD ADDRESS:

- Clear expectation of priests.
- Dialogue about sexuality including orientation at seminary.
- Compensation for priests across the diocese with alternative living situations.
- Revisit parochial vicar use instead of associate pastor.

## OPEN MICROPHONE

- New structures that assist us or create in us an atmosphere that makes and keeps us healthier.
- Task force needs ongoing dialogue to help us process the large amount of information that's been thrown at us.
- Awareness that the folks we serve need to be involved in our process and conversation.
- Task force is rather clerical as it stands now; maybe it would be helpful to expand the group to include others.
- Research into "holy orders" and the "priesthood of baptized" and the "whole history and concept of celibacy."
- Bishop Griffin of Columbus Letter on "expectations" might be a model for a priest-generated document and dialogue that would help us to reshape our lives.

- Emmaus experience hosted retreats to help us process—maybe retreats could help us to process this information and these issues.
- How do our living arrangements fit into our understanding of the experience of Church? Simply adjusting where you live does not affect one's relationship to the Church.
- We need clarity around words like "institution," "legalism" (referring to Bishop Pilla's remarks).
- Planning should take into account that there may be 50 percent fewer priests ten years from now.
- Five elephants (mentioned in Papesh's talk as out of our control) should be addressed because grassroots movements have changed our Church in the past. We still need to do that and say things that can cause the larger institution to know how we feel, how it is impacting us, etc.
- Should we as a presbyterate make a statement about what has been said here so that we might have a voice saying "we take responsibility and we ourselves are trying to address the effort to be better priests ourselves"?
- We need a structure and a methodology for the task force to hold the task force accountable and keep the presbyters included. Maybe a press conference would bring some life to it.
- The infirmed, aged priests of our diocese need more attention, visits, etc.
- I recommend a priests' newsletter to keep us included in the lives of priests, the sick, the "on leave," etc.
- Caution: Hasty comments from the task force, before we have processed this activity together with the lay faithful, may be harmful.
- A regular newsletter that keeps us informed has helped the Franciscan priests of our province.
- Let's not lose the sexuality piece. I sense that we are not talking about sexual orientation ourselves.
- The liberal-conservative dichotomy: How can we share and hear the other side in a more positive, growthful fashion?
- Those who left the priesthood and married have been left out of our conversation.

# Appendix 3. Summary: The Basic Plan for the Ongoing Formation of Priests

The following material is courtesy of the Diocese of Lansing, Michigan, from its Presbyteral Convocation of 2001. It was offered through Fr. Edward Estok of the Diocese of Cleveland at its Presbyteral Convocation of 2002. The *Basic Plan* divides the priest's life into five stages based on a constellation of events particular to each stage.

| #1 EVENT IN A PRIEST'S LIFE: DEPARTURE FROM THE SEMINARY | | | | |
|---|---|---|---|---|
| **Practical Tasks and Challenges** | **Temptations** | **Graces** | **Discernment** | **Programmatic Responses to Transition** |
| Bringing closure to seminary experience | Taking security from locking into familiar patterns, rigid legalisms | New beginning and growth | Identify resistances of the journey | Individual priests must be committed to ongoing change and growth |
| Leave-taking | | | | |
| Arrival | "Foreignness" of parish culture; a reactive stance toward life and people | Grace of vulnerability | Maintenance of a prayer life | Regular gatherings of newly ordained |
| Putting theory into practice | Self-doubt | | | |
| Appropriate a new identity | Finding one's role on the parish staff | | | First pastor- and priest-mentor |
| Relation to bishop and presbyterate | Difficult pastor, lack of privacy | Grace of community | Remaining in dialogue with community | Diocesan Director of Priestly Life |
| Celibate identity | Delusion of "self-sufficiency" | | | Spiritual Director |

| #2 EVENT IN A PRIEST'S LIFE: CHANGE OF ASSIGNMENT | | | | |
|---|---|---|---|---|
| **Practical Tasks and Challenges** | **Temptations** | **Graces** | **Discernment** | **Programmatic Responses to Transition** |
| Leaving with deliberateness | Discourage-ment, loss of heart | Participation in the paschal mystery | | Providing opportunities for sharing of experiences |
| | Refusal to adapt | | | |
| | Anger and resentment | | | |
| | Fear | | | |
| Moving graciously | | Renewal of one's commitment | How change is drawing us closer to God and how we respond | Providing opportunities for solitude |
| Beginning anew | Clinging attachment to previous experience | Extension of one's mission— broadening | Develop apostolic detachment | Appropriate breaks/ Religious retreat |

| #3 EVENT IN A PRIEST'S LIFE: FIRST PASTORATE | | | | |
|---|---|---|---|---|
| **Practical Tasks and Challenges** | **Temptations** | **Graces** | **Discernment** | **Programmatic Responses to Transition** |
| Form a relation with a particular place | Drawn to full-time administration | Exposure to God's grace alive in this people | What priorities is God drawing me to? | Provide skills and knowledge for manage-ment and administration |
| | Immobility or reactivity | | How are gifts of Spirit distrib-uted in this community? | Provide oppor-tunities for human and spiritual growth |
| | Lack of focus | Enhanced awareness of dependence on God's grace | What direction is Spirit giving to this parish? | Connections with persons of experience |
| Maintain relations with Bishop/ Universal Church | | Gratitude | | Establish priest/pastor-mentor |

| #4 EVENT IN A PRIEST'S LIFE: PRIESTS AT MID-LIFE | | | | |
|---|---|---|---|---|
| **Practical Tasks and Challenges** | **Temptations** | **Graces** | **Discernment** | **Programmatic Responses to Transition** |
| Reassessment of life's purpose(s) | Weariness of life | | New responses given experience, graces of life | Gatherings of peers |
| | Presumed self-sufficiency | | | Study of mid-life phenomena |
| | Interior fatigue (resigned disillusion) | | | Spiritual direction |
| Physical adjustment | Awareness of limits/mortality | Deeper self-knowledge | | Deliberate programs for integrating the facets of mid-life experience |
| | Waning energy | | Sift through options, priorities | Good medical consultation |
| Grief over losses/ reassertion of questions about celibacy (intimacy and connection) | Do something else before it is too late | Greater authenticity | | Senior-priest mentor program |
| Re-evaluate commitments and investments | Drawn to sadness, dis-couragement, isolated narrowness | More generous self-gift | Greater sense of self, Christ's need, God's direction | |
| Resurface concerns about intimacy and connection | View life from lens of disappoint-ment, anger, resentment | Life in communion: bishop, presbyterate, people, friends | How to deepen communion/ connections in faith, hope, and love | Mechanism for making contact with predecessors and successors |
| Plateaued-out: what is undone and what is undoable | | Greater self-acceptance | | |
| | Responsibilities to predecessors and successors | Renegotiate commitment and dedication | | |
| Spiritual: Take stock of place on the journey | | | | |

| #5 EVENT IN A PRIEST'S LIFE: SENIOR CLERGY STATUS | | | | |
|---|---|---|---|---|
| **Practical Tasks and Challenges** | **Temptations** | **Graces** | **Discernment** | **Programmatic Responses to Transition** |
| Integrating who one is and what one does for the sake of mission | Despair the past | Wisdom, insight | How to detach from past | Lectures and workshops on the dynamics of aging |
| Preparing to die | | Gift of focus, grasping what really matters | What to do with remaining time allotted | Personal and group counseling |
| Detachment from belongings and accomplishments | Lack of prospects for the future | | How to be present to faith community | Retreats, days of renewal, spiritual direction |
| Continuing to contribute to the life and growth of the Church | Loss of hope, despair | Hope | How to share experience of God's mercy | Public celebrations of senior priests |
| | | | Reappropriate celibacy | Specific roles at other communal gatherings (parish, diocese) |

# Appendix 4. The Organizational Life Cycle: Change Grid

Fr. Richard Rohr, O.F.M., offered this schema, which he called the "Change Grid," in a series of talks at the St. Paul Seminary School of Divinity of the University of St. Thomas in St. Paul, Minnesota, some years ago. The grid comes from the Management Design Institute of Cincinnati, Ohio.[1]

The grid gives the impression that the development and breakdown of an organization is a discreet, once and for all reality. The truth of organizational change is that it is a constant. The history of the Church, for instance, makes that abundantly clear. The undulating constancy of organizational change might be understood more clearly if the grid were seen in the context of the image below. Imposing the grid onto it, understanding the peaks and valleys to be reflective of a constant process, images organizational change more accurately than the grid alone.

---

[1] Used with permission of Fr. George Wilson, S.J., Management Design Institute, 110 E. 8th St., Cincinnati, Ohio 45202.

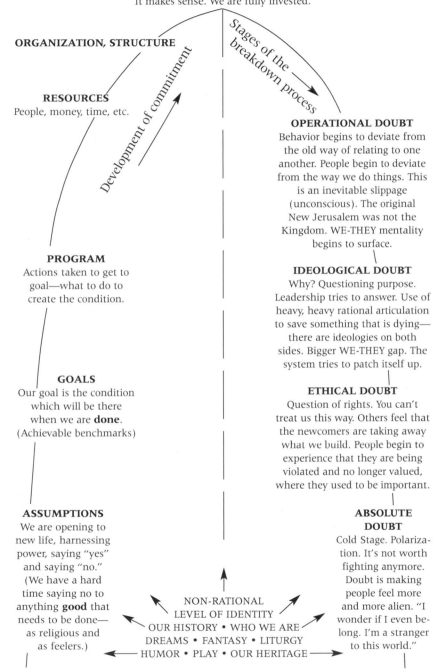

**CONSENSUS: WE!! NO DOUBT**
Total trust. I fit in. You fit in. We all know what we are about.
It makes sense. We are fully invested.

*Stages of the breakdown process* →

**ORGANIZATION, STRUCTURE**

*Development of commitment*

**RESOURCES**
People, money, time, etc.

**OPERATIONAL DOUBT**
Behavior begins to deviate from
the old way of relating to one
another. People begin to deviate
from the way we do things. This
is an inevitable slippage
(unconscious). The original
New Jerusalem was not the
Kingdom. WE-THEY mentality
begins to surface.

**PROGRAM**
Actions taken to get to
goal—what to do to
create the condition.

**IDEOLOGICAL DOUBT**
Why? Questioning purpose.
Leadership tries to answer. Use of
heavy, heavy rational articulation
to save something that is dying—
there are ideologies on both
sides. Bigger WE-THEY gap. The
system tries to patch itself up.

**GOALS**
Our goal is the condition
which will be there
when we are **done**.
(Achievable benchmarks)

**ETHICAL DOUBT**
Question of rights. You can't
treat us this way. Others feel that
the newcomers are taking away
what we build. People begin to
experience that they are being
violated and no longer valued,
where they used to be important.

**ASSUMPTIONS**
We are opening to
new life, harnessing
power, saying "yes"
and saying "no."
(We have a hard
time saying no to
anything **good** that
needs to be done—
as religious and
as feelers.)

NON-RATIONAL
LEVEL OF IDENTITY
OUR HISTORY • WHO WE ARE
DREAMS • FANTASY • LITURGY
HUMOR • PLAY • OUR HERITAGE

**ABSOLUTE
DOUBT**
Cold Stage. Polariza-
tion. It's not worth
fighting anymore.
Doubt is making
people feel more
and more alien. "I
wonder if I even be-
long. I'm a stranger
to this world."

← ← STASIS ← ←

# Bibliography

"Agreement with County Attorney Regarding Sexual Abuse of Minors." *Origins,* vol. 33, no. 5, June 12, 2003, 68–71.

Appleby, R. Scott. "Historical Overview: Priests in America, 1930–2002." *Origins,* vol. 33, no. 4, June 5, 2003.

———. "Surviving the Shaking of the Foundations: United States Catholicism in the Twenty-First Century." In Katerina Schuth, *Seminaries, Theologates, and the Future of Church Ministry: An Analysis of Trends and Transitions.* Collegeville: The Liturgical Press, 1999, 1–53.

Aschenbrenner, s.j., George A. *Quickening the Fire in Our Midst: The Challenge of Diocesan Priestly Spirituality.* Chicago: Loyola Press, 2002.

Baker, Andrew R. "Ordination and Same Sex Attraction." *America,* vol. 187, no. 9, September 30, 2002, 7–9.

Barrett, William E. *Shepherd of Mankind: A Biography of Pope Paul VI.* Garden City, N.Y.: Doubleday, 1964.

*The Basic Plan for the Ongoing Formation of Priests.* Washington, D.C.: The United States Catholic Conference, 2001.

Bausch, William. *Breaking Trust: A Priest Looks at the Scandal of Sexual Abuse.* Mystic, Conn.: Twenty-Third Publications, 2002.

Bernier, Paul. *Ministry in the Church: A Historical and Pastoral Approach.* Mystic, Conn.: Twenty-Third Publications, 1992.

Blanchette, Melvin C., and Gerald D. Coleman. "Priest Pedophiles." *America,* vol. 186, no. 13, April 22, 2002, 18–21.

Bolt, Robert. *A Man for All Seasons.* New York: Vintage Books, 1962.

*The Boston Globe* investigative staff. *Betrayal: The Crisis in the Catholic Church.* Boston: Little, Brown, 2002.

Bury, J. B. *The Invasion of Europe by the Barbarians.* New York: W. W. Norton & Company, 2000.

Cahill, Thomas. *How the Irish Saved Civilization: The Untold Story of Ireland's Heroic Role from the Fall of Rome to the Rise of Medieval Europe.* New York: Doubleday, 1995.

*Code of Canon Law.* Washington, D.C.: Canon Law Society of America, 1983.

*Common Bible: The New Revised Standard Version.* Atlanta: Thomas Nelson, 1990.

Cozzens, Donald B. *The Changing Face of the Priesthood.* Collegeville: The Liturgical Press, 2000.

—————. *Sacred Silence: Denial and the Crisis in the Church.* Collegeville: The Liturgical Press, 2002.

—————. "Time to Face the Facts." *The Tablet,* May 4, 2002, 8–9.

Dinter, Paul E. *The Other Side of the Altar: One Man's Life in the Catholic Priesthood.* New York: Farrar, Straus and Giroux, 2003.

Dolan, Jay P. *In Search of an American Catholicism: A History of Religion and Culture in Tension.* Oxford: University Press, 2002.

Dulles, s.j., Avery. *A Church to Believe In: Discipleship and the Dynamics of Freedom,* New York: Crossroad, 1982.

—————. *Models of the Church.* Garden City, N.Y.: Image Books, 1978.

—————. *Models of the Church: Expanded Edition.* N.Y.: Doubleday Image Books, 1987.

*Final Report.* Washington, D.C.: National Catholic News Service. *Origins,* vol. 15, no. 27, December 19, 1985, 446, 448.

Flannery, o.p., Austin, ed. *Vatican Council II: The Conciliar and Post Conciliar Documents.* Revised edition. Northport, N.Y.: Costello Publishing Company, 1992.

Gauthier, Mary L., ed. *Catholic Ministry Formation Enrollments: Statistical Overview for 2001–2002.* Washington, D.C.: Center for Applied Research in the Apostolate, Georgetown University, March 2002.

"General Instruction of the Liturgy of the Hours." *The Liturgy of the Hours According to the Roman Rite: Volume I.* New York: Catholic Book Publishers, 1975, 21–98.

Gibson, David. *The Coming Catholic Church: How the Faithful Are Shaping a New American Catholicism.* San Francisco: HarperSanFrancisco, 2003.

Guido, Joseph J. "The Importance of Perspective: Understanding the Sexual Abuse of Children by Priests." *America,* vol. 186, no. 11, April 1, 2002, 21–23.

Guller, Jon. "On 'Straightening Out' Catholic Seminaries." *America,* vol. 187, no. 20, December 16, 2002, 7–9.

Hebblethwaite, Peter. "Exit 'the people of God.'" *The Tablet,* vol. 240, no. 7596, February 2, 1986, 140–41.

—————. *Paul VI.* Mahwah, N.J.: Paulist Press, 1993.

Hellwig, Monica K. "Hope." M. Downey, ed., *The New Dictionary of Catholic Spirituality.* Collegeville: The Liturgical Press, 1993, 506–15.

Lakeland, Paul. *The Liberation of the Laity: In Search of an Accountable Church.* New York: Continuum, 2003.

Manning, Brennan. *The Wisdom of Tenderness: What Happens When God's Fierce Mercy Transforms Our Lives.* San Francisco: Harper/SanFrancisco, a division of Harper Collins publishers, 2002.

Martin, s.j., James. "The Church and the Homosexual Priest." *America,* vol. 183, no. 14, 1.

—————. "'To Love and to Pray': A Conversation with Boston's Archbishop Sean O'Malley." *America,* vol. 186, no. 13, October 27, 2003, 8–10.

Mendenhall, George. Gary Herion, ed. *Ancient Israel's Faith and History: An Introduction to the Bible in Context.* Louisville: Westminster John Knox Press, 2001.

Norwich, John Julius. *A Short History of Byzantium.* New York: Vintage Books, 1997.

*The Official Catholic Directory: Anno Domini 2003.* New Providence, N.J.: P. J. Kennedy & Sons, 2003.

O'Meara, Thomas F. *Theology of Ministry.* New York/Mahwah, N.J.: Paulist Press, 1999.

Papesh, Michael L. "Farewell to the Club." *America,* vol. 186, no. 16, May 16, 2002, 7–12.

Peters, Walter H. *The Life of Benedict XV.* Milwaukee: Bruce Publishing, 1959.

Pieper, Josef. *Leisure: The Basis of Culture.* New York: Random House, 1963.

Pollard, John F. *The Unknown Pope: Benedict XV (1914–1927) and the Pursuit of Peace.* New York: Geoffrey Chapman, 2000.

*Program of Priestly Formation.* Washington, D.C.: United States Conference of Catholic Bishops, 1993.

*Pseudo-Dionysius: The Complete Works.* Colm Luibheid, trans. *Classics of Western Spirituality.* New York: Paulist Press, 1987.

Ramsey, o.p., Boniface, trans. and annotator. *John Cassian: The Institutes. Ancient Christian Writers.* New York: Newman Press, 2000.

Ratzinger, Joseph. *Feast of Faith.* San Francisco: Ignatius Press, 1981.

—————. *Principles of Catholic Theology: Building Stones for a Fundamental Theology.* San Francisco: Ignatius Press, 1987.

—————. *The Ratzinger Report.* With Vittorio Messori. San Francisco: Ignatius Press, 1985.

Reese, s.j., Thomas J. *Archbishop: Inside the Power Structure of the American Catholic Church.* San Francisco: Harper and Row Publishers, 1989.

—————. *A Flock of Shepherds: The National Conference of Catholic Bishops.* Kansas City: Sheed and Ward, 1992.

—————. *Inside the Vatican: The Politics and Organization of the Catholic Church.* Cambridge, Mass.: Harvard University Press, 1996.

"Rite of Penance." *The Rites.* Collegeville: The Liturgical Press, 1990, 376–79, 335–46.

Rolheiser, o.m.i., Ronald. *The Holy Longing: The Search for a Christian Spirituality.* New York: Doubleday, 1999.

—————. "Same-sex Unions 'Harmful to Society.'" *Origins,* vol. 33, no. 11, August 14, 2003, 177, 79–182.

Schuth, Katerina. *Seminaries, Theologates, and the Future of Church Ministry: An Analysis of Trends and Transitions.* Collegeville: The Liturgical Press, 1999.

Steinfels, Peter. *A People Adrift: The Crisis of the Roman Catholic Church in America.* New York: Simon and Schuster, 2003.

Vacek, Edward. "'Acting More Humanely': Accepting Gays into the Priesthood." *America,* vol. 187, no. 20, December 16, 2002, 10–14.

Yamane, David. "The Bishops and Politics: Has the scandal stilled the church's voice? Don't believe it." *Commonweal,* vol. CXXX, no. 10, May 23, 2003, 17–20.

# Index